Judaism and the Gospel

Olaf Kovacek

ABSTRACT

This study explores the attractions that make for a successful ministry among Jews, and the hindrances that have impeded, and continue to impede, that mission. It begins with an overview of the theological, historical and missiological frameworks of this ministry, and then introduces the results of fieldwork done in Israel through interviews, case studies, observations, focus groups, and surveys, supplemented by other relevant literature that, altogether, forms a data base for strategizing future missionary work.

Non-believing Jews and Jews who had accepted Yeshua – so called Messianic Jews were asked what motivated them to either accept Yeshua as the Messiah or to reject him. From their responses the researcher has established a list of eighty-seven attractions. Among the most important inducements to conversion are: reading the New Testament, discovering Yeshua the Jew, and a witnessing friend or family member. Parallel with this list of attractions, the researcher has compiled a list of forty-five hindrances (theological, historical and sociological), among which are, most importantly: family opposition, fear of giving up one's Jewish identity, Christian doctrines (trinity, supersessionism…) and the Church's traditional anti-Judaism.

A second focus is on leadership. Here the researcher explores the differences between a secular and religious leader; the necessity of an effective training; and the need for contextual preparation, in which the Mission to the Jews is undertaken by persons who are equipped to effectively lead in a cross-cultural ministry and contextualized congregations.

This leads us to our third focus, on contextual issues. A ministry among Jews must be a contextualized ministry. It is supported in this study by a presentation of a positive view of Jews and a friendly Christian theology based on the awareness of the Jewishness of Yeshua, which is one of the first attractions for Jews.

This study concludes with recommendations and applications to leaders of the World Jewish Adventist Friendship Center, which minister to Jews. Jews don't lose their own Jewish identity in accepting Jesus but fulfill themselves in the Messiah, which, pragmatically, means retaining Jewish rituals that are compatible with Yeshua's message.

TABLE OF CONTENTS

TABLE OF CONTENTS vii

LIST OF ABBREVIATIONS xii

LIST OF TABLES xiii

LIST OF FIGURES xv

HEBREW-ENGLISH TRANSCRIPTION xvi

CHAPTER 1 INTRODUCTION 1
    Background 3
    Purpose 6
    Goals 6
    Significance 6
    Central Research Issue 7
    Research Questions 8
    Assumptions 8
    Delimitations 8
    Limitations 9
    Chapter Summary 9

CHAPTER 2 BIBLICAL FOUNDATION OF A MISSION TO JEWS ...11
    God is Love 12
    God Still Has a Plan for the People of Israel 13
    Missiological Framework 13
        Missio Dei (God's Mission) 14
        The Incarnational Ministry of God 14
    God's People Mission 16
        The Incarnational Ministry of the Church 16
        God's People: Mission Among Jews 17
        The Parting of the Ways 23
            Jewish Responsibility on the Parting of the Ways 23

    Christian's Responsibility on the Parting of the Ways ...27
     Supersessionism 27
     Rejection of the Torah 28
     Adversus Judaeos Literature 29
  Summary 34

CHAPTER 3 METHODOLOGY 35
  Literature Review 35
  Focus Groups 36
  Interviews 38
  Participant Observation 39
  Secondary Data 39
  Reliability and Validity 40
  Summary 41

CHAPTER 4 DATA: WHAT I FOUND 42
  Statistics About the Jewish People 42
    The World Jewish Population 42
    The World Jewish Messianic Population 47
    The Israeli Population 48
    The Israeli Messianic Population 49
  Focus Group 51
  Interviews 53
  Participant Observations 54
  Secondary Data 55
    Jews for Jesus' Survey 55
    Jewish Conversion in Literature 56
      Jews Converted to Catholicism 57
      Jews Who Converted to Evangelical, Protestant or
        Messianic Churches 59
  Analyzing my Data 60
    Findings as a Result of this Research 60
    Discovered Research Gaps 66
  Summary 66

CHAPTER 5 ATTRACTIONS AND HINDRANCES IN LITERATURE 71
  Attractions 71
    Respect for Yeshua's Life and Message 71
    Jewishness of Yeshua 72
    The New Testament 74
      How to Recognize the Words of Yeshua 76
      Yeshua and the Torah 77
      Yeshua's Authority 78
    Implications of these Attractions 79
  Hindrances 80
    Hindrances about Yeshua 80
      The Two Comings of the Messiah 80

    Universal Silence about the Ministry of Yeshua 81
    Yeshua's Purported Anti-Jewish Sentiments.................82
  Hindrances about the New Testament 83
    New Testament's Chronology 83
    Who Are the Writers of the Apostolic Writings? 83
    Use of the Hebrew Scriptures by the Apostolic Writings
   84
    The Messianic Prophecies...86
    Yeshua's Genealogy in Matthew 89
    The Virgin Birth of Yeshua 93
    The Trial of Yeshua 96
    Unity of God 96
    The Trinity and Incarnation 97
    The Apostolic Writings...104
  Historical Hindrances and Objection to Yeshua.......................107
    The Jewish Story of Yeshua, Toldot Yeshu..................108
    A Small Minority of Jews Accepted Jesus 108
    Excommunication of Yeshua...111
    Many Modern Scholars and Rabbis have Not Accepted
    Jesus 112
    Jesus Is Only One Among Many Other Messiahs 115
    The Role of The Church in the Suffering of Israel.......116
  Existential Hindrances and Objection to Yeshua.....................117
    Jews Are Very Proud of Their Culture and Attached to It
   117
    Challenging Supersessionism 122
 Summary 125

CHAPTER 6 LEADERSHIP IMPLICATIONS FOR JEWISH MINISTRY 126
  Leadership Principles...126
  Cross-Cultural Leadership 128
  The World Jewish Adventist Friendship Center........................128
    Jewish Ministry in the World..129
    Where Should We Encourage New Jewish Ministries? 130
    Consolidating the Existing Jewish Ministry 130
  How to Improve the WJAFC Work? 132
    Establishing a Sense of Urgency...................................132
    Second Coming of Jesus 133
    There is Still a Mission to Fulfill 133
    To Create a Coalition 134
  New Vision, Mission Statement and Strategy 134
    Qualities of a Good Vision and an Efficient Mission
      Statement...134
    WJAFC's Vision..135
    WJFAC's Mission Statement..135
    WJAFC's Goals and Objectives 135

       The Strategy 136
       Communicating the New Vision and Strategies 137
       Empowering Leaders and Church Members............................138
       Generating Short-Term Gains...139
       Consolidating Gains and Producing More Change...................140
       Anchoring New Approaches in the Culture.............................140
   Summary 141

CHAPTER 7 THEOLOGICAL AND MINISTERIAL IMPLICATIONS OF MY FINDINGS..142
   A Friendly Theology 143
       Discard all Negative Views on Israel.......................................145
       Positive Texts on Israel..148
           God Has Not Rejected Israel (Romans 9-11) 148
           The Covenant with Israel is Forever.............................150
           Israel Is Not Replaced by the Church 151
       Biblical Foundation of a Positive Theology Towards Jews......151
           Relations of Comfort Between Israel and the Church
              (Isaiah 40:1-5)...152
           Relation of Reconciliation Between Israel and the Church
              (Mal 4:5-6; Rev 11) 153
           Christian Declaration for Dialogue and Reconciliation 154
           Jewish Answers to Christian Statements 157
   A Contextualized Ministry...158
   Summary 161

CHAPTER 8 GENERAL CONCLUSIONS AND RECOMMENDATIONS ...162
   Recommendations for an Effective Jewish Ministry 163
       Jews do not Lose Their Jewishness 163
       Jews Complete Their Destiny in Jesus.....................................163
       They Should be Allowed to Practice the *Mitsvot*......................164
       Worshipping in their Own Context...165
       Jewish Practices are not Syncretism 166
   Summary 167

LIST OF ABBREVIATIONS

BIBLE

BHS-W4:	The Hebrew Bible used in this dissertation. *Biblia Hebraica Stuttgartensia,* used by permission.
NABC	New American Bible
NIV:	New International Version of the Bible. The Bible I will use mostly
JPS	Jewish Publication Society, Jewish Bible.
LXX	Septuagint cf. Glossary.
TNIV	Today New International Version of the Bible

CHRONOLOGICAL DESIGNATIONS

BC	Christian way to designate the years Before Christ
AD	Christian way to designate the years after Christ Anno Domini
CE	Common Era, designate the years after Christ
BCE	Before Common Era, designate the years before Christ

DICTIONARIES AND COMMENTARIES

NIBC	New International Bible Commentary
NIDOTTE	New International Dictionary of Old Testament Theology and Exegesis.
BDB	Brown, Driver and Briggs Hebrew-English dictionary

OTHER ABBREVIATIONS

CRI	Central Research Issue
WJAFC	World Jewish Adventist Friendship Center, a study center of the General Conference of the Seventh-day Adventist Church dedicated to study the best way to reach Jews and implement successful models of Jewish Evangelism.
SBL:	Society of Biblical Literature. This society was founded in 1880 to foster biblical scholarship and published in cooperation with Hendrickson as a handbook of style for biblical scholars and writers. This will be followed for all biblical Hebrew-English transcription.
SDA:	Seventh-day Adventist Church

HEBREW-ENGLISH TRANSCRIPTION

Since I am going to use some Hebrew nouns or names, I will transcribe them in English for this dissertation. I have chosen to follow the recommendation of the Society of Biblical Literature (SBL) manual for this transcription (Alexander 1999, 28).

א	alef	ʼ	כ/ך/כּ	kaf/khaf	k, kh	שׁ	shin	sh
ב/בּ	bet/vet	b, v	ל	lamed	l	שׂ	sin	s
ג	gimel	g	מ/ם	mem	m	ת	tav	t
ד	dalet	d	נ/ן	nun	n			
ה	he	h	ס	samekh	s			
ו	vav	v	ע	ayin	ʼ			
ז	zayin	z	פ/פּ/ף	pe	p, f			
ח	Chet	Ch	צ/ץ	tsade	ts			
ט	tet	t	ק	qof	q			
י	yod	y	ר	resh	r			

CHAPTER 1

INTRODUCTION

Since the time of Yeshua[1] and Paul, the Jewish people have been a major concern in evangelism for the church. In the gospel of Matthew, after listing the names of the twelve disciples, it is written, "These twelve Yeshua sent out with the following instructions: 'Go nowhere among the Gentiles, and enter no town of the Samaritans, but go rather to the lost sheep of the house of Israel. As you go, proclaim the good news, the kingdom of heaven has come near'" (Matt 10:5-7)[2]. When Yeshua spoke with the Canaanite woman he was even more radical, "I was sent only to the lost sheep of the house of Israel" (Matt 15:24). Yeshua had great compassion for the Jews of his time (Matt 9:36; Matt 14:14; Matt 15:32; Matt 20:34). In another passage, he cried over the city of Jerusalem, comparing his attitude to the city to that of a mother towards her children (Luke 19:41). And when he gave the great commission Yeshua spoke first of Jerusalem and Judea (Acts 1:8).

In the same way, Paul and the disciples were motivated to share the gospel with Jewish people. Even though the Apostolic Writings and the church have traditionally portrayed the gospel mission as one shared between Paul and Peter, Paul being the apostle of the Gentiles and Peter the apostle of the Jews (Gal 2:7), the most beautiful and moving text about Jewish evangelism is the famous pericope written by Paul in his letter to Rome (Rom 9-11).

---

[1] In this dissertation, I refer to Jesus by the literal transcription of his name in the Gospels
[2] Unless otherwise noted all texts are taken from the New International Version of the Bible.

However, in the period after the death of the last apostle, the Church Fathers built an anti-Judaic church. "A whole body of anti-Judaic literature was produced in the second century condemning the Jews socially and theologically" (Bacchiocchi 1977, 178). In essence, the leaders of the Christian community kept the Jews away from the Church.

While there were Jews in the Middle Ages who accepted the Messiah, there was no sympathetic mission to the Jews after the golden age of the first century conversions until the beginning of the nineteenth century, when Christian agencies were established to reach Jews. The CMJ (Church Ministry among Jews) was created in London in 1809 with the help of three famous visionaries: William Wilberforce, Charles Simeon, and Lord Shaftesbury (CMJ 2008-2010). According to Mitch Glaser, "The Church of Scotland established their own mission board to reach the Jews in 1825" (1984, 103). On the Catholic side, the big shift occurred in 1842, when Marie-Alphonse Ratisbonne, a French Jew who was converted through a miracle, and his brother, who had been converted to Catholicism before him, founded the Congregation of Notre Dame de Sion. Marie-Alphonse subsequently moved to Palestine in 1850 and stayed there until his death in 1884, founding the Jewish-Christian Study Center in Jerusalem, known today as the Ratisbonne Monastery, which was devoted to witnessing to the Jews.

However, the paradigm shift in the Mission only appeared later, in the second half of the 20th century among Christians, after the crimes of the Holocaust became public knowledge. Christians began to recognize the Jewish people's right to be called God's people, and this motivated the Evangelical part of the Christian community to witness to the Jews and to help them to discover Yeshua as the Messiah of Israel. Over the last 30 years, numerous independent Messianic communities have arisen to promote a contextually sensitive approach to Jewish evangelism and outreach (Dauermann and Spielberg 1997, 17).

The Messianic movement has branches wherever there are large Jewish communities: in Israel, in Europe, in the United States of America, in the former Soviet Union, in South America, South Africa, and Australia. Even though converted Jews have longed formed a part of various Christian communities, today the great majority of Jews who accept Yeshua join Messianic congregations.

In this dissertation I intend to study what attracts and what hinders the proclamation of the gospel to the Jews from a mission-centered viewpoint. The problem I am pursuing is the following: what are the elements in Christian theology that most attract Jews to Yeshua, or lead to his rejection? Is a contextually sensitive ministry more efficient and attractive to the Jewish people than the traditional evangelistic approach? The purpose of this dissertation is to create a new model of evangelism to present Yeshua to the Jewish people.

Background

In writing this introduction for the dissertation, I must include my own experience and ministry, which gives abundant evidence of the Lord's guidance and goodness to me. It has been my intention for a long time to work on a doctoral degree, but the Lord waited for me to have experience first in working specifically for the Jews.

My family background is highly pertinent to the subject of this dissertation. I was born into a Jewish orthodox family. I started to learn Hebrew when I was six years old, went to a rabbinical school (*Yeshiva*) for my primary education, and worshipped in the synagogue almost every Sabbath. I became *Bar-Mitsva*—Son of the commandment —by a religious service when I was 12 (just as Yeshua did in Luke 2:42). At that time I was sure that I was in the right faith and felt that to be a practicing Jew was the best way to serve God.

It was during my teenage years that I began to talk to Christian people about God. Finally, when I was 18, I made the decision to accept Yeshua (Jesus) as my personal Savior and to be baptized by immersion.

Very soon after baptism I chose to be engaged in the proclamation of the gospel to the world, and especially to the Jewish people. My specific mission was triggered by a visit I made to Israel in 1975 with Liliane, my wife. This was my first visit to Israel, and my first confrontation with the situation of the church there. Before that trip, I had never even considered being a pastor; at that time, I was an accountant, intending to go on to get a master's degree in accounting. However, when I saw the situation of the church in Israel, the very few Jews who were in contact with authentic Christians and their ignorance about Yeshua, the Lord through his *Ruach Hakodesh* (Holy Spirit) put a very strong conviction in my heart. I turned to Liliane, weeping and full of emotion, and said, "I think that I must become a pastor, for the Lord is calling me to work here among Jews." At that time, she certainly did not realize the meaning and implication of these words, but for me the decision was definitive. I could not turn my back on the *Ruach Hakodesh,* and since that day I have devoted myself to presenting Yeshua to the Jews.

Returning home, I found I had no interest in accounting any more. One year later, after consulting with my pastor, I entered the seminary to study theology and prepare myself for the ministry.

There were not many Jews in those days within the Seventh-day Adventist Church, either in France or in Israel. The Messianic movement was not as developed in the 1970s as it has become since. When I first accepted Yeshua, I found, to my great surprise, a Messianic church in Paris. Yet I could see, on my first visit, that the congregation had lost their specific Jewish culture. They were, for instance, worshiping on Sunday, meaning that they rejected one of the most important worship components of the Jewish Bible: to worship on Sabbath in honor of the creation of God. Conforming to mainstream church practice, they had lost what it means to be a Jewish believer in Yeshua.

That is why I joined the Seventh-day Adventist Church, which was, as I understood it, the closest Christian denomination to the Jewish people and to the Bible. Today, 37 years later, I find that it is still difficult for Jews to become Seventh-day Adventists in spite of all the points they have in common.

Even though my first years of ministry were among regular Christian people, I always had a desire in my heart to do something special for the Jewish people. In every city where I ministered I made contacts with the rabbis and the Jewish community. I tried to involve rabbis in my ministry, especially when I was in a city where our church was involved in a radio ministry. I would ask the Rabbi to prepare some radio programs with me for a Jewish audience, which would always turn out to be successful.

After ten years of regular ministry, I felt that the time had come to develop a ministry for the Jewish community. At that time, this was a novel idea: all Seventh-day Adventists pastors were "generalists" working for the community as a whole, and little thought was given to specific missions. This was the dawning of the PC and Internet era, and I seized the opportunity to use this relatively cheap technology to publish and distribute a new magazine on Jewish-Christian dialogue. It was not easy to convince the leadership of my church in France to sponsor such a project, but with the help of a Jewish-Adventist friend, Jacques Doukhan, a well recognized scholar among Adventists, the magazine took shape and was printed. It was an immediate success. I was even invited by France's national television to speak about the purpose of this magazine in noon news broadcast, reaching millions of television viewers.

After seven years of ministry with the magazine, which we called *L'Olivier*, I was called by the Church to go to Israel to lead the national Seventh-day Adventist Church there. Four years later, the General Conference of Seventh-day Adventists, based in the

United States, asked me to lead the World Jewish Adventist Friendship Center. The Center is dedicated to Christian-Jewish dialogue to promote Jewish-Adventist communities around the world. To this end, it creates material and trains leaders for this specific mission. So it was that after 21 years of ministry, my 1975 calling to present Yeshua in Israel was confirmed. I knew from my own experience how to speak with Jews about accepting Yeshua in continuation with Jewish practices. However, I felt I needed more formal education in order to improve my missionary abilities and the capacity to work inter-culturally. That is why in 2005, following the advice of my good friend, Jacques Doukhan, I applied to Fuller Seminary for a Master of Arts, which would include leadership and missiology. Today, after seven years of hard studies I am ready to defend this dissertation for a doctoral degree in Jewish evangelism.

Purpose

My purpose in this study is to show how Jews perceive Yeshua, and using that perception, to show how Yeshua can best be presented as the Messiah to this community.

Goals

The goal of this study is to create a successful, practical model of evangelism directed towards Jews that will help Adventist leaders working in a Jewish ministry, especially those associated with the World Jewish Adventist Friendship Center (WJAFC).

Significance

As the director of the World Jewish Adventist Friendship Center, I have long thought that we need better heuristics to direct our mission. I have designed this research to create such a heuristic. I believe that it will allow us to improve our mission to the

Jewish community. The WJAFC is a component of the Office of Adventist Mission at the General Conference of the Seventh-day Adventists. I have worked there for 12 years. My experience in promoting the Gospel in Israel goes back 15 years. This background has given me certain insights that I have tried to distill into this dissertation.

The Seventh-day Adventist church has been present in the territory now known as Israel for more than 100 years. There were around one thousand members in the church in Israel when I left the country in 2012, spread out among 25 congregations. In my opinion, the Seventh-day Adventist church has not yet reached the point of being an indigenous church there.[3] I hope that my work will help Adventists and other Christians to understand the local culture and how to reach the *Sabra*—native Jewish people. The gospel message in Israel becomes more of a living, immediate thing when it is something Jews share with other Jews. I have thus focused on what attracts Jews and what hinders them when Yeshua is presented to them. Some factors are theological (the divinity of Yeshua, God, and so on) and cannot be avoided, even if they do need a clear biblical grounding. Other factors, however, are sociological or missiological, and can be corrected. My thesis is that Jews need to understand that Yeshua is not foreign to the Jewish people but one of them.

I have seen Jews join the Yeshua movement in the spirit that prompted so many of them to make that choice in the first century. It is crucial to reconnect the message of Yeshua to Jewish culture and practices to open this path again.

Central Research Issue

The Central Research Issue is to identify what attracts or hinders Jews in Israel from accepting Yeshua as the Messiah in order to find the best way to share Him.

---

[3] An indigenous church which is able to own their own symbols and rituals that can be understood by the local people, and is owned and led by local people and not by foreign leaders anymore (Oxford 2005).

Research Questions

The research questions that I pose in this dissertation are:

1. What do today's Jews feel about Yeshua?
2. What attracts or hinders Jews from accepting Yeshua?
3. According to the testimony of converted Jews, what were the obstacles in the way of accepting Yeshua?

Assumptions

Yeshua said, "I am the way and the truth and the life. No one comes to the Father except through me" (John 14:6). In Acts it is written. "Salvation is found in no one else" (4:12). Believing these words, my first assumption is that Jews need Yeshua for their salvation.

My second assumption was that the Hebrew Scriptures and the Apostolic Writings, together called Old and New Testament, constitute the Bible and are both the authentic word of God.

My third assumption is that it is possible for Jews to accept Yeshua and remain culturally Jews.

Delimitations

The temporal coordinates of my research project are defined by the modern era (which includes the state of Israel and the history of anti-Semitic atrocities that led up to that state). Geographically, the Jews that I interviewed were mostly from Israel. This research is therefore delimitated to Israel.

My research is not comparative, so I have not included non-Jewish communities in my fieldwork.

Limitations

I began this research while living in Israel, but in March 2012 I moved to France, which made it difficult to effect closure on some elements of the research. To make up for this gap, I extended my research to include dimensions of the worldwide Jewish presence to reinforce my mission strategy proposals that, I contend, should be the focus of the World Jewish Adventist Friendship Center.

There is a wide spectrum of beliefs, denominations, and level of practice among the global Jewish community. American Jews are very different from Israelis Jews, for instance. American readers should keep these differences in mind while reading this dissertation.

Chapter Summary

Chapter 1 is an outline and summary of the direction, purpose and significance of the dissertation. In Chapter 2, I provide the biblical and theological frameworks I am using for a ministry of Jewish outreach. In Chapter 3, I present the research methodology used in this study. In Chapter 4, I provide the data and the conclusion of my findings. Chapter 5 is a literature review, organized according to the framing problems that any mission to the Jews concerned with spreading the message of Jesus has, historically, encounter, and will encounter in the future. In Chapter 6, I apply these findings to the mission strategies chosen by the World Jewish Adventist Friendship Center and its leadership, suggesting appropriate changes in its operation and tactics. In Chapter 7, I present the theological and missional case for what I am calling a friendly presentation of Jesus and a critical contextualization in Jewish Christian congregation. Chapter 8 contains my conclusion and lists recommendations for an effective Jewish ministry.

This chapter has introduced my personal background and motivations for this research. Since I am myself a Jewish believer in Yeshua, I want to know what attracts and hinders other Jews from accepting this belief. Since I belief the message of Yeshua is necessary for salvation, I wanted to know how best to share Yeshua with my fellow Jews. In this chapter I have presented the purpose, goals, and questions of my research. My expectation in this research is grounded on my perception that so far, the Christian mission to the Jews has not been very successful, but that it can be. It is possible to present Yeshua to the Jewish people in such a way that the message breaks through the barriers thrown up by the history of Christian anti-Semitism, and that members of the Jewish community realize that Yeshua does fulfill the law and the prophets. This dissertation shows the biblical grounding for creating a mission to the Jewish community that would present Yeshua in Jewish terms, and then suggests possible strategies to implement it.

CHAPTER 2

BIBLICAL FOUNDATION OF A MISSION TO JEWS

In this chapter, I present the biblical and theological reasons for the fact that sharing the gospel with the Jewish people requires a special mode of evangelism. Biblically, Israel is not one nation among many nations, but God's beloved. From the time of the Patriarchs to today, God has steadfastly loved Israel (Rom 11:28).

This theme is essential to understanding the whole dissertation. I will contend that the failure of the church during her history to convert the Jews stems from a pattern that emerged and hardened between the second to the fourth century. The failure of the proclamation of the gospel to the Jews today still echoes the mistakes that the patristic church made back then.

The first part of this chapter will develop the theme of God's love for Israel. The second part applies the theological concept of *missio Dei* to the Jewish people. The Mission of God will be defined, and it will be shown how God and Yeshua fulfilled their mission among the Jews. The third part examines the success of the mission among the Jews of the first century, comparing this to the failure in the following centuries for reasons that will emerge in my analysis. The fourth part of this chapter will develop a specific mission plan towards the Jews, emphasizing a context-sensitive practice. "The work for the Jews, as outlined in the eleventh chapter of Romans, is a work that is to be treated with special wisdom" (Nichol, Cottrell, and Neufeld 1955, 1079). This "special wisdom" consists in cultural understanding and respect. This chapter ends on a pastoral

God is Love

The relationships between God and Israel are characterized by love. In the Tanakh, the Tetragrammaton YHWH is pronounced when God renews his covenant with Israel after the golden calf sin in Exodus 34:6-7, when God renews His covenant with Israel in terms of love (Exod. 34:10).

In the history recorded in Exodus, Israel often fails, which is why the people are condemned to wander before they reach the Promised Land. Nevertheless, Israel remained the people of the covenant. This pattern will be repeated many times throughout the history of Israel. That is why at the end of the wilderness experience, just before entering the Promised Land, God said again that Israel has been chosen not because she is better than the other peoples but because of the promise God has made with the Patriarchs (Deut. 7:6-8) God had chosen Israel not because Israel was better or more numerous than any other people but because "God is love" (1 John 4:8) and God wanted to be faithful to his promises to the patriarchs.

In the Apostolic Writings we have the same affirmation of God's love (John 3:16; 1 John 4:8), and God's unconditional love for Israel (Rom 11:28). Why would God still love Israel when they have rejected Yeshua? Paul answers: "For God's gifts and his call are irrevocable" (Rom. 11:29). It is clear that Paul, in line with Deuteronomy 7, sees God's love not as the result of Israel's merits, but rather as an unmerited gift that is "irrevocable." That is why "God did not reject his people" (Rom. 11:1-2). Great missiologists agree with this Pauline doctrine: the new covenant has not replaced the "old" one.

Jews would also rightly contend that the covenant God ratified at Sinai is forever settled in heaven. It is eternal and unending. It is no wonder, then, that down through the centuries Judaism has utterly repudiated any idea of a 'new' covenant that regards God's earlier covenantal activity as 'old' (Glasser et al. 2003, 18).

Meditating on this love of God, Rabbi Wyschogrod says, "The uniqueness and unsubstitutability of God's love for Israel turns out to be the guarantee of God's fatherhood toward all persons, elect and non-elect" (cited by Soulen 2004, 23).

God Still Has a Plan for the People of Israel

Luke's story of the encounter between some of the disciples and Yeshua at Emmaus after Yeshua's crucifixion is key to understanding the continuity between the God of love of Israel and the God of love proclaimed by Yeshua: "And beginning with Moses and all the prophets, he interpreted to them in all the scriptures the things concerning himself (Luke 24:27). It is on the basis of this story that we know that even today, God still has a plan for his people, Israel (Hos 3:4-5). As Paul writes, God's plan for Israel (Rom 11:23) is to be grafted "again" on their "own" olive tree. As Glaser writes, "Indeed the tenth chapter of Romans expressly speaks of the conversion of Israel through the medium of missionary preaching" (Glaser 1985, 113).

Missiological Framework.

Reaching the hearts of the Jews is a continuation of the mission God begins in the Tanakh, and is taken up by Yeshua in the Apostolic Writings. Given the context of this mission—God's especial love for Israel—it is important to reflect seriously on the historical missiological handling of this mission. Here, I wish to describe its aspects: the Mission of God, Yeshua's mission through his incarnation, and the work of Yeshua's disciples. Finally, using Yeshua's ministry as a model, I want to emphasize the necessity of an incarnational ministry among his people.

Missio Dei (God's Mission)

Etymologically the word *missio* is the Latin word for "mission" which means "sending" (Wright 2010, 149), and *Dei* is "God." For, missiologists and theologians, *Missio Dei* is about God's "sending" of messengers to spread the news of the salvation of humanity. David Bosch as defines this mission of God:

> God's self-revelation as the one who loves the world, God's involvement in and with the world, the nature and activity of God, which embraces both the church and the world, and in which the church is privileged to participate. *Missio Dei* enunciates the good news that God is a God-for-people (Bosch 2006, 10).

The mission in the Hebrew Scriptures is the mission of God. As Bosch put it, "A careful reading of the Old Testament thus reveals the enormous missionary significance of Yahweh's dealing with Israel" (Bosch 1993, 5). This original mission has a double aspect: God's mission towards Israel, and Israel's God-given mission among the nations. When Israel closed herself in a particularism, God forced Israel to fulfill her mission through suffering and the Babylonian and Roman exiles.

The Incarnational Ministry of God

The *missio Dei* continues in the Apostolic Writings, but in a Trinitarian mode. Johannes Nissen points out that "John's Gospel is one of the strongest biblical supports for the understanding of mission as *missio Dei,* that is the movement of God to man, in creation, in incarnation and redemption, a movement involving Father, Son and Holy Spirit" (2007, 89). The gospels affirm 39 times that God sent Yeshua. Yeshua, further, sent the Holy Spirit and his disciples.

Incarnation was the first missionary act of Yeshua (John 1:1, 14). After ministering throughout Israel's history to build his people, God ultimately comes to earth as a simple man (Phil. 2:5-8). The first purpose of God in the incarnation was to reveal himself (John 1:18). Coordinately, Yeshua is the Savior. "He was the Redeemer before as after His incarnation. As soon as there was sin, there was a Savior" (White 2002, 210).

Yeshua's ministry was a double-sided act: reconciling God and humanity (2 Cor 5:19) and reconciling Jews and Gentiles. "The reconciliation of Jews and Gentiles must be seen as prototype (or model) for the reconciliation of other groups. Galatians 3:28 expresses the early Christian vision that all existential divisions are overcome in Christ" (Nissen 2007, 137).

Yeshua was incarnated within a culture and a people. He was born in Bethlehem as a Jew from Jewish parents who belonged to the tribes of Judah and Levi.[1] He was named for one of the great heroes of the Bible time, Yehoshua (Joshua). As with many biblical prophets, his ministry was presaged in his name: YaHWeH will save. As Pinchas Lapide asserts, "The Christian community has its roots in Judaism. Jesus lived and taught within the Jewish people. He himself as well as his disciples and the apostles were Jews; they partook of the faith and the history of their people" (1975, 488). Calvin Shenk also expresses very well this affirmation:

> Jesus was clearly a Middle Eastern Jew. He was born in the line of David to a Jewish mother. He was circumcised and taken to the Temple at age 12. He observed the Sabbath, Passover, Feast of Tabernacles, and Hanukkah. ... He confined his ministry mainly to Jews. When he died he was described as "King of the Jews" (2001, 405).

Yeshua is shown to be a fully practicing Jew in the Gospel, including, as Shenk remarks, a participant in Jewish rituals. For instance, in Matthew, we see him being

---

[1] According to the gospels of Matthew and Luke, the ancestors of Yeshua were from the tribe of Judah, and in the Gospel of Luke Myriam, his mother, visited her relatives, the parents of Yochanan (John) who were Levites. Zachariah was even officiating in the Temple when he was visited by the angel.

questioned by the Rabbis to become *bar-mitsva*—son of the Commandments, when he was 12. We see, in Luke, how he had garnered such respect and reputation that when he visited his family's synagogue in Nazareth, he was invited to read the Torah and to give a *drasha,* a sermon on the text of the haftara (Luke 4:16-20). "Moreover, it seems clear that Jesus thought of his Jewish brothers and sisters as God's elect people. They, not the Gentiles, were the chief beneficiaries of his ministry. Though he occasionally healed non-Jews, he apparently understood that he had been sent first of all for Israel's sake" (Koenig 1979, 26-27). And in fact the first mission given by Jesus to the disciples was a Jewish mission (Matt. 10:5–6).

God's People Mission

Yet it is in Matthew, too, that we can distinguish a decisive broadening of the mission, for in the Great Commission passage, where the resurrected Christ commands his followers to reach every nation, tribe, and language (Matt 28:19-20). In Paul, this is the basis for the injunction to demonstrate the wisdom of God to all rulers and authorities (Eph. 3:10). The function of Yeshua's disciples, to be witnesses, is the same as the one given to Israel in the Tanakh (Isa. 43:10) (Wright 2010, 168). The broadening, contrary to the latter tradition in the patristic Church of the 2nd century, did not abolish the special status of the Jews. The Jewish people were a priority in the mission given by Yeshua (Acts 1:8), as affirmed by Paul (Rom. 1:16). Jews were the most receptive people, knowing the scriptures and awaiting the Messiah. The gospel was first preached in Jerusalem.

The Incarnational Ministry of the Church

Donald McGavran defines the mission of the church as "any good activity at home or abroad which anyone declares of being the will of God" (McGavran 1977, 241).

"At home" and "abroad" are key terms, here. But wherever the mission is implemented, Yeshua's example must govern it. That example corresponds to the incarnational dimension of the Mission, which is "the ability to take the meanings of the faith story and make them real in society outside the congregation" (Bozeman 1995, 140). Yeshua's incarnation conveyed the message of God to the world; similarly, Yeshua's messengers must incarnate in their world and society the "good news" —Gospel— outside the congregation, among the people, in their cultures. "Incarnational mission refers to the fact that Jesus' act of taking on humanity is a model for missionaries in their practice of adapting to local culture" (Pocock, Van Rheenen, and McConnell 2005, 328). As missionaries we need to incarnate ourselves—choosing our re-birth— into a new context. Pocock, Van Rheenen and McConnell say missionaries "cannot enter as newborns, but they can learn the language and the culture of their new context in such a way that they can behave like those who were born in the culture" (2005, 15). The application of this incarnational mission to the Jews in the 1st century was relatively clear-cut: the disciples were Jews, born in Israel or into a Jewish family, and tacitly understood themselves as Jews. The difficulty, at that time, was the ministry to the Gentiles. Today, the terms have reversed, and an incarnational (contextualized) mission to the Jews is now required, in Paul's spirit.

God's People: Mission Among Jews

Presenting the Mission in the New Testament, Nissen argues that the mission or the "sending" was summarized in this way in the gospel of John,

> (1) John the Baptist is sent by God to testify about Jesus (1:6-8; 3:28); (2) Jesus himself is sent by the Father to testify about the Father and do his work (4:34; 17:4 etc.); (3) the Paraclete is sent by both Father and Son to give testimonies about Jesus; (4) and, finally, the disciples are sent by Jesus to do as he did (20:21; 17:18) (McPolin 1969, Nissen 2007, 76).

The progression from 1 to 4 is clear. God sends two agents of change and transformation into the world: (a) John the Baptist and (b) Yeshua. Then Yeshua sends two agents of change and transformation into the world: (a) the Holy Spirit and (b) the disciples.

The disciples were Aramaic-speaking Jews, who attended the synagogues, temples, and Jewish worship services, knew the Jewish people and Jewish culture as their family and friends. Being Jews themselves, they conveyed, to the Jewish community, their transformation through Yeshua in terms consistent with their own Jewish culture. They followed Yeshua's order (Acts 1:8) by starting in Jerusalem and Judea, and preached the gospel first to the Jewish people.

The book of Acts, "which chronicles the early days of the Church" (Schoeman 2003, 55), describes the church's mission in the first century. The first chapters of Acts are exclusively devoted to the mission of the disciples in Jerusalem and Judea. Chapter 9 represents a major turning point in the Church's history: the conversion of Saul, who became Paul. Paul was literally named the "apostle of the Gentiles" (Rom. 11:13; Gal. 2:8), but in every city to which he came, he went first to the synagogues: in Antioch (Acts 13:14), in Iconium (Acts 14:1), in "Thessalonica (Acts 17:1-2), in Berea (Acts 17:10), in Athens (Acts 17:17), in Corinth (Acts 18:4), in Ephesus (Acts 18:19), and in Corinth during his next trip (Acts 19:8). Paul knew that conversions in the Jewish community would attract the thousands of "God-fearing" people who were at the edge of the Jewish community.

The book of Acts shows that this strategy was a great success. In Acts 2, Peter preached and it is said that 3,000 people (Jews) responded positively and were baptized (Acts 2:37-41), not only 3,000, it is also said, "the Lord added to the church those who were being saved" (Acts 2:42-47) and the text adds "daily." Three thousand Jews was a small number, but it was an excellent beginning. In Acts 2 it is shown that most converts were made among the Jews who came as pilgrims for the feasts (Passover, Pentecost, or Shavuot), but afterwards returned home, where they could spread the word. Thus, the church continued to grow. In chapter 4 it is written, "But many who heard the message believed, and the number of men[2] grew to about five thousand" (Acts 4:4), giving us an increase of the congregation in Jerusalem alone to more than 5,000 people. Acts 4 – 6 relates the exponential growth in numbers, all in the Jewish community. We are told that those who were against Yeshua were the priests and the Jewish leaders, but in Acts 6:7 it is affirmed that even the priests accepted Yeshua as the Messiah. "So the word of God spread. The number of disciples in Jerusalem increased rapidly, and a large number of priests became obedient to the faith." From these chapters of Acts, we can estimate the number of the disciples increased in Jerusalem to more than 10,000.

In Acts, the scene then shifts to Paul's ministry, which, as we said, was centered in the synagogues among the Jewish diaspora in the Eastern Mediterranean. In Iconium "a great number of Jews and Gentiles believed" (Acts 14:1). "They received the message with great eagerness (Acts 17:11). In Corinth "Crispus, the synagogue's ruler, and his entire household believed in the Lord" (Acts 18:8). This did arouse the opposition of many Jewish leaders, but we should not over-emphasize that opposition:

> It is likewise important to notice that the resistance Paul meets in the synagogues of Pisidian Antioch, Iconium, Thessalonica, Corinth, and Ephesus is more than balanced out by the successes of the gospel, which begins with the day of Pentecost and continues all the way to Paul's witness in Rome, where some Jews were convinced by what he had to say (Acts 28:24). The initial proclamation in Jerusalem not only let to acceptance by great numbers of persons, it extended into the priestly families and Pharisaic circles (Seifrid 2008, 33).

When Paul gave his report to the church, all the believers were amazed to see how many thousands of Jews believed in Yeshua (Acts 21:20). This number naturally shaped

---

[2] At that time only men were counted in religious gatherings, which means the real numbers were much higher than what the book of Acts tells.

the 1st century Church: "At its inception the Church was entirely Jewish. All of the very first members of the Church—the apostles, the disciples, and the center and heart of the church, the blessed Virgin Mary—were Jews" (Schoeman 2003, 51). Ray Register, who has lived in Israel and written a book about the modern church planting movement in the Holy Land, writes: "Archeological evidence abounds in Jerusalem and Galilee indicating that numerous synagogues eventually became churches, and thousands of Jews received Jesus as their Messiah and became 'Nazarene[3]'" (2000, 4). This long eclipsed episode of Church history is now better known. Pawlikowski provides a summary from the Scriptural and archaeological evidence:

> (a) The movement begun by Jesus and continued after his death in Palestine can best be described as a reform movement within Judaism. There is little extant evidence during this period that Christians had an identity separate from Jews. (b) The Pauline missionary movement, as Paul understood it, was a Jewish mission that focused on the Gentiles as the proper object of God's call to his people. (c) Prior to the end of the Jewish war with the Romans that ended in 70 CE, there was no such reality as Christianity. Followers of Jesus did not have a self-understanding of themselves as a religion over against Judaism. A distinctive Christian identity only began to emerge after the Jewish-Roman war. And (d) the later sections of the New Testament all show some signs of a movement toward separation, but they also generally retain some contact with their Jewish matrix (2011, 28).

There are countless confirmations of the Jewishness of the first church. "We are convinced that the communities to whom the four Gospels were written still very much considered themselves Jewish" (Allen and M.Williamson 2004, XXV). Most of the scholars date the writing of the gospel in the second part of the first century or even the beginning of the second century. Jacques Doukhan affirms:

> In the beginning, it was possible for a Jew to be a Christian without having to deny his or her Jewish roots, without having to leave his or her alma mater. As we just saw, a significant amount of biblical, archeological, and

---

[3] "Nazarene" or Notsrim is the Hebrew name of Christians, this name comes from the fact that they believe that Yeshua from Nazareth was the Messiah.

> sociological evidence suggests that until the fourth century Jews by thousands and hundreds of thousands were joining the "new" faith. And until then, Jews and Christians were living together in the same religious community (2002, 33).

Today, the visitor to Israel can see the many cities where Jews and Christians peacefully co-existed and intermingled. One of the best examples is the town of Capernaum, owned by the Catholic Church today. It is interesting that when entering the town, the first big building we see is the 20th century octagonal church that was built on "piles" or columns, in order to preserve the archeological discoveries that are still visible under it. There, "Peter's House" can be seen (blue arrow in Figure 1). After the departure of the disciples for their worldwide mission, the Yeshua-believing Jews used Peter's house as a house of prayer, the first house of prayer in Capernaum. A few hundred meters from this site (just behind it in Figure 1), a huge ruin can be seen with several rooms and columns. This was the synagogue of Capernaum (red arrow) built in the 4th century (see Figure 2).

From the first century to the fourth century, Yeshua-believing Jews of Capernaum met and worshiped in the "house of Peter," which was a house of prayer, and Jews who did not believe in Yeshua met and worshipped in their regular synagogue. The town had about 1,500 inhabitants, and one imagines they met together for feasts and family celebrations such as circumcision, presentation of babies, bar-mitsva, marriage, and funerals. They went to the same *mikve* for the ritual immersion; they were part of the same religious community even if they had their own Rabbis. We have no trace in Capernaum of any conflict between these two groups of people.

FIGURE 1

SYNAGOGUE AND HOUSE OF PRAYER IN CAPERNAUM.

FIGURE 2

SYNAGOGUE BUILT UPON THE REMAINS OF THE "SYNAGOGUE OF JESUS."

The Parting of the Ways

However, the success of the mission to the Gentiles spelled doom for Jewish evangelism. Gentiles with no connection to the Jewish community began to distance the church from the Jewish people. An anti-Jewish discourse sprang up. This separation between Israel and the Church is theologically called the "Parting of the Ways." As Pawlikowski points out, "The growing number of biblical scholars who have become engaged in this 'Parting of the Ways' discussion all stress the great difficulty in locating Jesus within an ever-changing Jewish context in the first century" (2011, 29). Doukhan sums up the current consensus: "The Jewish Christian separation was, indeed, a complex process. And it would be presumptuous to believe that we can reach a clear and definitive view of what actually happened" (2002, 33).

Jewish Responsibility on the Parting of the Ways

For a long time it was generally accepted that two factors initiated by the Jewish people were at the origin of the "parting of the ways." The first factor was the supposed indifference of Yeshua-believing Jews to the fall of Jerusalem in and their refusal to fight the Romans in 70 CE, for which Jewish leaders called them out. The second was their supposed indifference during the second war against Rome in 132-135 CE. However, today many scholars doubt this story. Jewish Christians were not alone among the Jews in rejecting the war: so did the Pharisees.

To understand the 21st century situation of the mission to the Jewish community, we have to glance at the history of Christian-Jewish relations, and especially the fruits of the breakdown of those relations in the third or fourth century. Those fruits were evil: the terrible persecutions of the Jews, and the drying up of the Christian mission to the Jews. These historic themes impinge largely on the Mission to the Jews even today.

The "parting of the ways" is a story of mutual culpability and misunderstanding. On the Jewish side, the traditional story is that the Rabbinical Council of Yavneh, which met after the Romans sacked the Temple in Jerusalem in 70 CE, expelled Jewish Christians. The council wrote a curse against the Nazarim (Nazarenes), which was read against the *Notsrim* (Christians), this curse was included in the *Birkath Ha-Minim* (a curse upon Heretics), in the *Amidah* or eighteen benedictions.

> The Eighteen Benedictions is the title given to the central prayer which is said three times a day by all observant Jews. It is also known as the *Shemoneh Esreh* ('Eighteen'), the *Tephillah* ('Prayer'), or the *'Amidah* ('standing') because one stands to say this prayer (Instone-Brewer 2003, 24).

In the second place, they excluded Yeshua's followers from the synagogue:

> In the course of time, probably in the eighties of the first century, the Jewish prayer known as the Eighteen Benedictions was expanded to include an extra section in which Christians ("Nazarenes") and heretics (minim) were anathematized. From that moment Jewish Christians, many of whom had continued their participation in the Jewish synagogue worship, were irrevocably excluded from it (Bosch 1984, 19).

Georgi thought that by the beginning of the second century, "Jews and Christians began to develop their own identities; not only against each other but also against the huge range of other options available to them both. These options were suddenly considered deviant" (Georgi 1995, 65).

Some have seen traces of this decree of exclusions from the synagogue in the gospel of John, which was written after Yavneh[4] (John 9:22; 12:42; 16:2). However this reading assumes that Yavneh was significant for the whole Jewish community, rather than the Rabbinically governed part, Shaye Cohen points in his essay that the Yavneh Rabbis were concerned to produce "a society which tolerates disputes without producing sects" (Cohen 1984, 29). The result was the Mishnah, the spirit of which is captured in

---

[4] The gospel of John was written at the end of the 1st century, between 95 and 100 CE

the tannaitic midrash remark: "Do not make separate factions (*agudot*) but make one faction all together" (1984, 29). Thus, no group could separate itself from the community under the premise that it alone held the truth (Cohen 2010, 47). Given what we know, the immediate effect of Yavneh has been exaggerated. Certainly the rift remained among factions that were militantly against Rome (Zelotes) and others that did not want to fight Rome, considering that this could threaten the survival of Israel.

The Eighteen Benedictions or Amidah prayer exists today in the prayer book of all Jewish denominations or groups. Traditionally, the composition of these texts is dated to the time of Ezra, leader of the Great Assembly.[5] According to Instone-Brewer: "The general consensus is therefore that the Eighteen originates from the Second Temple period, though we do not now have access to any version which existed before the Temple was destroyed" (Instone-Brewer 2003, 27).

The Eighteen Benedictions or *Amidah* includes the *Birkat Haminim* (curse of the heretics), which is the twelfth prayer. We have several versions of the *Amidah*, the oldest being Palestinian and Babylonian. Versions have also been found in the Genizah of Cairo (fragments T-S K27.33D and T-S K27.33b). The *Birkat Haminim* reads, in English:

> For the apostates, let there be no hope and may the kingdom of the arrogant be quickly uprooted in our days; and may the *Nazarim* and *Minim* instantly perish; may they be blotted from the book of the living, and not be written with the righteous. Blessed are you Lord, humbler of the arrogant (Instone-Brewer 2003, 31).

This old version uses the Hebrew word *mashumadim* to mean "apostates." However, as Steven Katz summarizes the current state of research, the "malediction created at Yavneh did not include the term *Notzrim*" (2006, 287). Our evidence from this

---

[5] The Great Synagogue is also known as the Great Assembly. The Jewish tradition especially the Talmud and the Pirke Abot say that the Great Assembly was established during the Persian period by Ezra (Neh. 8-10), and was the religious Jewish authority during the rest of the Persian period. It is believed that Haggai, Zechariah, and Malachi were members of this Great Assembly, but the book of Ezra mentions also Ezra, Zerubbabel, Jeshua, Nehemiah, Mordecai, and Bilshan (Ezra 2:2), in Leviticus Rabba they are called "Ezra and his companions" (2:11).

period comes from Christian rather than Jewish sources. In Jerome, the claim is made that the curse on the Christians was pronounced three times a day. Tertullian (Tertullian 2004, (Adv Marc. 4.8.1) 24) and Augustine in his letter 112 to Jerome (quoted by Instone-Brewer 2003, 31) also claim that the official Jewish position was to curse Christians. These early Christian testimonies, then, seem to fail in three ways: (a) they are biased; (b) they are inconsistent; and (c) they do not conclusively link the sectarians named to Jewish Christians. This does not mean that the curse might not have been propounded, but not systematically. The evidence shows that the *birkat hanimin* was extremely flexible

In the modern version of the amidah, the English reads:

> Let there be no hope for informers, and may all the heretics and all the wicked instantly perish; may all the enemies of Your people be speedily extirpated; and may You swiftly uproot, break, crush and subdue the reign of wickedness speedily in our days. Blessed are You Lord, who crushes enemies and subdues the wicked (Siddur Tehillat Hashem 2012).

The apostates of the old version became the "informers", which, it is believed, reference those who betrayed the Jews to the Romans. Again, here there is no official curse of the Nazarim, but instead a curse against those "enemies" who would divide the Jewish community. The Hebrew word *'oyvekha,* for enemy, is uttered in the modern version, along with the word for the "heretics" *minim.* As Jacques Doukhan concludes:

> Recent scholarship ... established on the basis of semantic, stylistic, and historical evidence that this curse was a pre-Christian origin. There are good reasons to think the word "Christians" (*notsrim*) was later added to the word "heretics" (*minim*), around the third or the fourth century (2002, 36-37).

Today, while most of the Jewish denominations have included in their Siddur the *Amidah*, the Conservative and Reform movement omits the 12th blessing or *Birkat Haminim* to make the *Amidah* more universal (Petuchowski 1968, 214-215). It is a beautiful prayer, and one that I see no harm in recommending for use to Jewish Adventist congregations.

Christian's Responsibility on the Parting of the Ways

The early Christians used a Greek translation of the *Tanakh* called the *Septuagint*, which was made around the 2nd century BCE. These writings produced what is called the New Testament, or Apostolic Writings. The last Apostolic book is the gospel according to Yochanan (John), one the closest disciples of Jesus, written between CE 90 and 100.

The Christian church of the second century thus looked at its Jewish roots through a Greek prism, which reflects the church's Hellenistic context. "The universal use of the Greek language and culture permitted the early evangelists to communicate the gospel clearly to everyone in the empire" (Fanning 2009, 7). The prevailing Hellenistic ethos moved the church far away from the original Hebrew culture of the *Tanakh*. The fathers of the church were fluent in Greek; they read, studied, and meditated in Greek and through ancient Greek philosophers (Clark 1947, 33). The concepts developed in Greek philosophy were incorporated by the fathers of the church into orthodox doctrine by the fourth century, changing the liturgy, organization of the church, and the doctrine.

The three major doctrinal changes relevant to this chapter occurred between the 2nd and the 4th centuries. (1) The church introduced the Marcionite concept of supersessionism or "replacement theology" (some say "displacement theology"). (2) The church codified the rejection of the Torah of Moses. (3) Finally, a number of doctrines that collectively froze in place the parting of the ways were issued by the Council of Nicaea in 325. Symbolically, the first act of the Council was to "set a date for Easter distinct from the Jewish Passover thereby effectively separating Jews and Christians" (Amos 2010).

Supersessionism

Prioritizing the Gentiles in her preaching, the church's relationship with Judaism turned darkly negative. By the 2nd and 3rd centuries, the early fathers of the church, who came from Gentile backgrounds pronounced and wrote many anti-Jewish statements that fueled Christian anti-Semitism, or what Jules Isaac has called "the teaching of contempt" (Isaac 1964).

Marcion was a Christian leader who hated Jews and everything related to Israel and the Hebrew Scriptures and advocated a total divorce between the church and Israel. He denied that the God of the *Tanakh* was the father of Yeshua, and denied altogether Jesus' human nature. He edited the *Apostolikon* (Pauline epistles), and the *Euaggelion* (gospels) to reflect his doctrine. "Marcion's theology was dominated by the antithesis between the Old Testament Creator God of Law (the Demiurge) and Jesus' God of love and grace" (Head 1993, 310). Marcion applied his antitheses systematically: between the church and Israel, between the Jewish Sabbath and the Christian Sunday, between grace and law, and so on. Although excommunicated in 144 CE, by the 5th century certain of his *antithesis* had become fixed in church doctrine and attitudes. To him we owe the notion that the church was the *Verus Israel*, the "true Israel" (Simon 1996), in which the Israel of the Law was superseded by the "New Covenant" or New Testament. Constantine officially replaced the Jewish Sabbath by the Christian/pagan Sunday under the influence of supersessionism, and this shaped the future history of the church.

Rejection of the Torah

For the Jewish community, when the Council of Nicaea's replaced the biblical Sabbath by the pagan Sunday, the church became alien in form and content to the Torah and its commandments. To be Christian, at this point, one could not continue to be Jewish. The Council of Nicaea ignored the teaching of Yeshua, who was all his life faithful to the Torah and the teaching of the prophets and continually affirmed them in the gospel (Matt. 5:17). In the parting of the ways, Christians forgot Yeshua incarnational message.

The rejection of the law by the church had already begun in the second century. The Torah had been the Bible of the first century church, and as long as the church was composed of a majority of Jews, it continued to be faithful to it.

The Sabbath bound together the Messianic community. Yeshua did not abolish it. Today, Messianic Jews are reclaiming Yeshua's vision. The Sabbath has been so important during the Jewish history that Achad Ha-Am, the father of cultural Zionism said, "More than Israel has kept the Sabbath, the Sabbath has kept Israel" (Cited by Eisenberg 2004, 128).[6] The introduction of new doctrines and pagan traditions between the second and the fourth century put up a wall between the Jewish people and the church and Yeshua, theologically ghettoizing Jews in the Christian empire.

Adversus Judaeos Literature

The church bears another responsibility for the parting of the ways and for inciting the Jewish rejection of Jesus by producing and encouraging Adversus *Judaeos* literature, creating a massive anti-Semitic discourse.

As was pointed out above, Acts and the Pauline letters show that the Jews massively accepted Jesus before the destruction of Jerusalem. This movement could have continued if the church had continued to lovingly preach a God who "loved so much the world that he gave his son" to save it, instead of adopting a hateful, antagonistic anti-Semitism, or a less hateful but still un-Pauline supercessionism. What should have been a loving relationship became a strong enmity. The church of the second century became an exclusivist organization that took the destruction of the Temple and the defeat of Rabbi Akiba and Bar Chochba in 132-135 CE as a confirmation of God's withdrawal from Israel. A body of Christian literature is known as *Adversus Judaeos Literature* and

---

[6] The original source of this sentence from Achad Ha-Am was published in the magazine *Hashiloach*, created by the philosopher in 1896. This quotation, is from the volume iii page 6, but difficult to find today.

refers to a corpus "of Christian polemical texts specifically directed against the Jews, which were written from the first century to at least the 18th century CE" (Paget 2008, 6).

In this corpus of texts, that of Justin Martyr (100-165 CE) stands out as "the most important and comprehensive anti-Judaic document" (Pawlikowski 2008, 19). It is in the form of a dialogue with Trypho, who could be identified with Rabbi Tarphon[7] of the Tannaitic period. Justin Martyr defended the idea that God no longer had a covenant with the Jewish People, that the Gentile church replaced Israel and God would be dealing with them only in His plan of redemption.

Ignatius, the bishop of the church at Antioch (50-117 CE), ruled that anyone caught celebrating Passover with the Jews would be considered as partakers with the killers of Christ and the apostles.

Tertullian (160-220 CE) wrote a tractate "Against the Jews" where he affirmed that because the Jewish people under the influence of the Pharisees rejected Jesus, the whole Jewish race was responsible for the death of Jesus, being thus subjected to divine wrath. This became an all too common motif in the history of the Christian-Jewish interaction.

Eusebius of Caesarea (260-339 CE) argued "that Jews are responsible for their own fate, blaming them for the death of Jesus" (Fryš 2008, 149). He also wrote, "Jews are always cursed by God, and thus doomed to perpetual punishment."

Eusebius wrote in the shadow of the most important turning point in the history of the Church: the conversion of Constantine in 313 CE. Constantine, it could be said, also "converted" the church—into an extension of the empire, as the official religion. Constantine mixed religious attacks on the Jews and anti-Jewish laws, as for instance in

---

[7] A Tanna is of the generation that followed the destruction of Jerusalem. His leadership at the beginning of second century could be the basis for the famous Trypho figure of the dialogue of Justin Martyr.

329, when he signed a decree to forbid Jews from harassing converts to Christianity (Linder 1987, 124-132).

The rhetoric of John Chrysostom (350-407 CE) shows how far the church had fallen away from Paul's vision. In his *Adversus Judaeos* in 386-387 CE, he accused the Jews, past and present, of deicide, a claim that was to become central to the *Adversus Judaeos* tradition and official Christian teaching for centuries" (Kessler 2008, 92). In one of his sermon he writes:

> The Jews are the most worthless of all men. They are lecherous, greedy, rapacious. They are perfidious murderers of Christ. They worship the devil, their religion is a sickness. The Jews are the odious assassins of Christ and for killing God there is no expiation possible, no indulgence or pardon. Christians may never cease vengeance, and the Jew must live in servitude forever (Rydelnik 1999, 283).

The inversion of Yeshua's message could not be more complete. However, much more influential was Augustine, generally considered to be the greatest theologian of the ancient church. His remarks about the Jews are found in the commentary to the Psalms, the polemic against the Manicheans, and the City of God. In the commentary on the Psalms he approved of the Marcionite notion that the covenant with Israel had passed to the Church after Jesus's crucifixion:

> They raged and crucified Him: and afterwards began to see miracles wrought in the Name of Him Crucified; and they trembled still more that His Name should have so much power, since when in their hands He seemed unable to work any; and pricked at heart, at length believing that there was some hidden divinity in Him whom they had believed like other men, and asking counsel of the Apostles, they were answered, "Repent, and be baptized every one of you in the Name of our Lord Jesus Christ.[8].

Since then Christ arose to judge those by whom He had been crucified, and turned away His Presence from the Jews, turning His Presence towards the Gentiles... Finally,

---

[8] http://www.ccel.org/ccel/schaff/npnf108.ii.CXXXII.html#fnf_ii.CXXXII-p30.2 (accessed on January 15, 2013).

in the City of God, he created a grand narrative on the theme of the Christian City of God against the City of the Devil, with the Jews figuring, after the resurrection of Christ, as a witness people. In continuity with his commentary on Psalm 59:11 "But do not kill them [the Jews], O Lord our shield, or my people [the Christians] will forget. In your might make them wander about, and bring them down." Augustine devised the foundational story for the church regarding those Jews who did not convert:

> The rest are blinded, of whom it was predicted, Let their table be made before them a trap, and a retribution, and a stumbling-block. Let their eyes be darkened lest they see, and bow down their back always. Therefore, when they do not believe our Scriptures, their own, which they blindly read, are fulfilled in them, lest perchance any one should say that the Christians have forged these prophecies about Christ which are quoted under the name of the sibyl, or of others, if such there be, who do not belong to the Jewish people. For us, indeed, those suffice which are quoted from the books of our enemies, to whom we make our acknowledgment, on account of this testimony which, in spite of themselves, they contribute by their possession of these books, while they themselves are dispersed among all nations (quoted in Dyson 1998, 890).

This history sets the stage for the paranoid attitude towards the Jews common in Europe after the fall of the Roman Empire. Put on the defensive, Jews were put in the position of having to say "no" to Jesus in order to survive as a community. This "no" was directed at the Jesus who had been constructed by the Church Fathers. This, unfortunately, became the image of Jesus preached by a Gentile church. Clark Williamson sums up the church's responsibility for "the parting of the ways" and the Jewish "no" to Jesus:

> The Jewish "no" is quite real, but it was a "no" to a displacement ideology of the covenant; a "no' to a spiritualized and dehistoricized understanding of redemption emptied of its this-worldly promises of the end of oppression, war and injustice; and a "no" to the claim that salvation was now the property of gentiles and accessible to Jews only on condition that they turn their backs on the God of the Exodus and Sinai. Of the God who displaces Jews with gentiles and abrogates the covenant made with Israel, Martin Buber comments: "When I contemplate this God I no longer

recognize the God of Jesus." The Jewish "no" was a "no" to an invitation to join a church that defined itself as a gentile (not a Jewish) people, as a universal (not a particular, Jewish) people, as a spiritual (not a carnal, Jewish) people, as a replacement (not a replaced, Jewish) people, and as a superior (not an inferior, Jewish) people. This Jewish "no" to the gentile church's ideological distortion of its own gospel results from a firm decision to remain faithful to the God who had liberated Israel from oppression and who promised someday so to liberate and redeem not only Israel but all the world. Jews could only reject a church whose message denied the validity of the covenant of Sinai and the importance of a dual fidelity to that covenant—the fidelity of Israel to Torah and covenant and the fidelity of the God of Israel to the Israel of God and to God's gracious promise (Williamson 1993, 975).

The story that the church triumphed from the second to the fourth century is only true in a worldly perspective. For the Jewish people, and for the Jewish Yeshua, it was a disaster. I myself as a Jew don't see with positive eyes what happened in these foundational centuries of the church. Whether Constantine's conversion was sincere or fake and only political, it created misery for the lovers of the Bible, and the doctrines stemming from Constantine's church compromised the church and the throne, and sealed the parting of the way from the Jewish people and also from the authentic teaching of the Bible. Alan Hirsch, speaking about the conversion of Constantine, puts it well: "This shift to Christendom was thoroughly paradigmatic, and the implications were absolutely disastrous for the Jesus movement that was incrementally transforming the Roman world from the bottom up" (2006, 60). Rodney Stark adds:

> Far too long, historians have accepted the claim that the conversion of the Emperor Constantine (ca. 285-337) caused the triumph of Christianity. To the contrary, he destroyed its most attractive and dynamic aspects, turning a high-intensity, grassroots movement into an arrogant institution controlled by an elite who often managed to be both brutal and lax (2003, 33)

Since the massive Jewish disengagement from Yeshua's message and the acceptance of Yeshua as the savior in line with Jewish tradition occurred mostly in the 4th

century, it behooves us as bearers of the mission to the Jews to understand what happened in the history of the church at that time.

Summary

The biblical framework of this research is crucial to understanding why Yeshua could be preached in terms of a Jewish ministry, as a Jewish messiah, and to find a way to be effective in this ministry. Christians must apprehend God's love for the Jewish people and His plan for their salvation without falling back on a supersessionist theology that has no real Biblical standing. In order to save His people God started His ministry a long time before the incarnation of Jesus; in fact his plan started before the foundation of the world (John 17:24), and it is the definition of the *Missio Dei*. This mission of God had to be continued by His people, but due to contingent historical factors and certain powerful influences in the early church, the church ceased preaching God's love to Israel and the mutual misunderstanding caused a strong separation that was called the "parting of the ways". The understanding of this historical fracture will help also to understand the research presented in the next chapter.

CHAPTER 3

METHODOLOGY

I used multiple research methods to understand what separates Israeli Jews who believe in Yeshua from those who do not. The selection of people for this research was done through a network of relationships. I built a network of Jewish and Messianic ministers and friends who were able to put me in contact with suitable participants for my focus groups and interviews. This is called in qualitative sociological research "snowball sampling" by Earl Babbie:

> This procedure is appropriate when the members of a special population are difficult to locate... In snowball sampling, the researcher collects data on the few members of the target population he or she can locate, then asks those individuals to provide the information needed to locate other members of that population... (2009, 208).

I have made a demographic study in order to define the target population, first the world Jewish population and then specifically the Israeli population in order to know better the composition of messianic congregations.

I included a demographic cross-section in my interviews of men and women, youth and adults, native Israelis and Jewish immigrants to Israel to get the broadest sense possible of the hindrances and attractions to accepting Yeshua.

Literature Review

Since the Messianic Movement has become larger, a number of rabbis and scholars have written and published literature on topics related to it. The literature review for this dissertation was key in understanding what Jewish scholars think about Yeshua. Surprisingly, many of them (Flusser, Ben Chorin, Lapide, Buber, and so forth) are extremely positive about Yeshua. The literature review also helped me understand the rabbinic rejection of Yeshua as the Messiah or as a Jew.

Focus Groups

A focus group is usually a group of five to eight people who meet to discuss or interact on a specific topic. Rosaline Barbour defines it qualitatively: "Any group discussion may be called a focus group as long as the researcher is actively encouraging of, and attentive to, the group interaction" (Barbour 2007, 2). My research conformed to the model described by Viggo Søgaard: "A focus group is a group depth interview with a small group of people. It is conducted by a trained moderator, and the interview is loosely structured" (Søgaard 1996, 107). The fact that the group is focused "implies that the interview is limited to a small number of issues" (Stewart, Shamdasani, and Rook 2007, 37).

The cohesiveness of the groups was essential for success in this kind of research. The research suggests that cohesiveness is enhanced by bringing together people of similar backgrounds and attitudes. "This does not mean that focus groups should consist of people who agree perfectly with one another, but it does suggest that groups composed of individuals with violently opposed opinions will be troublesome" (Stewart, Shamdasani, and Rook 2007, 26).

In June 2010 I began the focus group phase of my research by creating a group composed of Messianic Jews who all belonged to the Seventh-day Adventist Church in Israel.

I had hoped to gather another contrasting focus group of Jews who do not believe in Yeshua. Unfortunately, here I ran into several roadblocks. I could not find anyone even willing to help me gather these participants for my research purpose.

As an example of the historically conditioned hostility that my research is, in a sense, about, I adduce the case of the interview I did with a well-educated man who had written many books and has many friends in Israel. He was happy to let me interview him. I spoke to him about gathering a focus group, and gave him the consent form I had prepared. Hours later, this man sent me an email not only refusing to participate in this research, but requesting that I delete my interview of him from my computer. Speaking with him later, I discovered that he had believed I was asking his opinion as an expert, not recruiting him into my focus group set. I told him that my purpose was to know what he thought about the person of Yeshua. It was at this point that the interview was cancelled.

Strengths of a focus group are: (A) the potential of creating a good interpersonal dynamic, in which disagreements do not lead to anger, but instead to the emergence of clarified themes and self-understanding; (B) the creation of a comfortable atmosphere permits members of the group to debate and voice issues they might not discuss individually; and (C) the neutralizing of the fear of proselytizing, since the group is structured so as to allow people to speak their mind without any one view dominating.

There is a weakness in focus groups in as much as cohesiveness might inspire some to censor their views. For instance, a Jew who is a hidden believer might be disinclined to frankly state what he thinks. In Israel there are biases against believing in Yeshua that might intimidate some. That's why the focus groups have to be followed up with personal interviews.

Interviews

Interviews were the most important part of my research, and are at the core of qualitative research in general. Doing an interview according to Kvale is an "attempt to understand the world from the subject's point of view, to unfold the meaning of peoples' experiences, to uncover their lived world prior to scientific explanations" (2007, xxviii). This was my main reason for interviewing a variety of Jews.

The interviews helped me understand different trends within the Israeli population and their perceptions of Yeshua. Even though I carefully prepared the questions I wanted to ask, I conducted them as "unstructured interviews," by which I mean that I felt free to ask more questions based on the interviewee's answers. Russell Bernard says that "unstructured interviewing can be used for studying sensitive issues, like sexuality, racial or ethnic prejudice, or hot political topics" (2006, 213). Given the sensitivity of the Yeshua mission in Israel, I felt comfortable opting for this interviewing format.

By the end, I had managed to interview some non-believers: an Orthodox Lubavitcher Jew; an Orthodox Jew involved in anti-missionary work; a traditional Jew; a secular Jew; and two rabbis, one man (a Traditional Jew) and one woman (a Liberal Jew).

There are unique strengths in interviewing people on a one-to-one basis: (A) It is a very good way to ask personal questions; and (B) unstructured interviews with open-ended questions allow a freer back and forth, giving a more rounded view of the interviewees world views. The weaknesses are: (A) that people may contour their responses to what they think the interviewer wants to hear, and (B) the interviewer can subconsciously distort the session by urging a subjective point of view in a tone that stifles the flow of conversation.

Participant Observation

Participant observation is a key instrument in ethnographic fieldwork in order to understand the real-time practices and customs of a specific group. In my research, I have used this method to observe a traditional Jewish synagogue, a Messianic congregation, and an Adventist-Jewish congregation. Participant observation is "intentionally unstructured and free flowing" and "flexible" (Leedy and Ormrod 2010, 147).

I attended the synagogue, messianic congregation, and Adventist-Jewish congregation in order to look for the potential obstacles confronting new Jewish converts in attending a contextualized service. Even though I identified myself with these groups, I wanted to gain an understanding of the complexities of these three groups in Israel.

One of the strengths of participant observations is that to observe worship for an ethnographic study gives more objective information than participating as a worshipper or preacher. I observed three different kinds of worship (regular Jewish, Messianic, and Jewish Adventist).

The weaknesses are first it is a time-consuming process, and it is inherently difficult to document, since it is forbidden to take notes or to record anything on the Shabbat. As a researcher, then, I had to write my observations afterwards, to the best of my ability. The record I made is inevitably incomplete.

Secondary Data

I have used secondary data to confirm or to refute my findings by others testimony. Thus, I tried to listen to as many life experiences as possible in order to discover how people came to Yeshua, or the reasons people refused the message. I know that some Jews who had accepted Yeshua left the church after some period of time, and I was curious to discover why. I developed many of my case studies through a literature review on the topic of conversion, using protestant and catholic books, which I found useful to compare with the real life experiences of my interviewees.

Reliability and Validity

The question of reliability and the validity of the data of qualitative research connect with two different points:

- The "consistency and trustworthiness of research findings" (Kvale 2007, 122). Kvale raises the issue of consistency by asking if the findings are reproducible at other times, by other researchers.
- The transcription and interpretation (analysis) of the interviews. It is important that trust and confidence be built between the interviewee and the interviewer. The validity of the findings is directly related to the matter of correctness and truth in the statements.

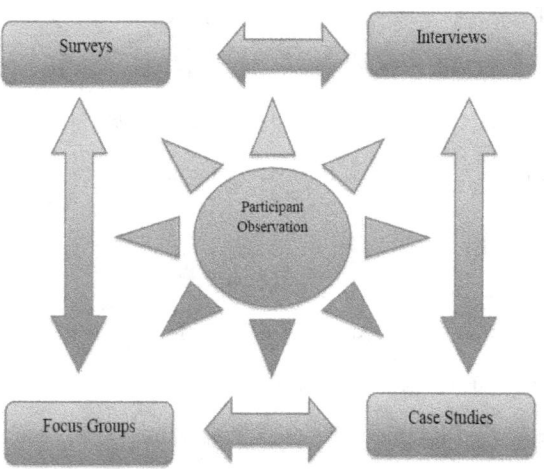

FIGURE 3

INTEGRATION OF RESEARCH METHODS

A common method to check reliability and validity is triangulation or in this case quadrangulation, which verifies the credibility of the answers and findings by comparing them to at least three sources or methodologies used in the qualitative research.

Summary

In this chapter I have described the methodology of the research I conducted in Israel. After listing the demographic figures of the Messianic movement in Israel, I have related my literature review to the data I gathered from a survey, a focus group, interviews, and participant observations. To facilitate this comparison, I drew on case studies from secondary data from my literature review as well. In the following chapter I am presenting the findings and data.

CHAPTER 4

DATA: WHAT I FOUND

After describing the methodology of my research, I want to share here the heart of my findings, which derive a focus group I have led, interviews, participant observations and secondary data from a survey done by Jews for Jesus and the literature review. The latter, it is important to note, were not experiential, but developed from cases found in the literature review I made of protestant and catholic books concerning the mission to the Jews.

Statistics About the Jewish People

The Jewish American Committee annually publishes a book with statistics (American-Jewish-Committee 2010, 75). They estimate the world Jewish population as between 13 to 14 million people.

The World Jewish Population

However, even though it is difficult to answer the question "who is Jew?" and therefore to have exact numbers, I found that the Jewish population of the twenty largest countries totals more than 15 million.

TABLE 1

TWENTY LARGEST JEWISH POPULATIONS

Rank	Country	Population	Jews	% in country	% of diaspora
1	United States	310,000,000	6,500,000	2.10%	43.33%
2	Israel	7,900,000	6,000,000	75.40%	38.00%
3	France	63,000,000	600,000	0.95%	4.00%
4	Canada	34,000,000	400,000	1.18%	2.67%
5	United Kingdom	63,000,000	300,000	0.48%	2.00%
6	Russia	140,000,000	250,000	0.18%	1.67%
7	Argentina	41,000,000	200,000	0.49%	1.33%
8	Germany	82,000,000	120 000	0.15%	0.80%
9	Australia	21,000,000	110,000	0.52%	0.73%
10	Brazil	195,000,000	100,000	0.05%	0.67%
11	Ukraine	45,000,000	80,000	0.18%	0.53%
12	South Africa	51,000,000	75,000	0.15%	0.50%
13	Hungary	10,000,000	50,000	0.50%	0.33%
14	Mexico	110,000,000	40,000	0.04%	0.27%
15	Netherlands	17,000,000	40,000	0.24%	0.27%
16	Belgium	11,000,000	35,000	0.32%	0.23%
17	Italy	60,000,000	30,000	0.05%	0.20%
18	Chile	17,000,000	25,000	0.15%	0.17%
19	Switzerland	7,600,000	20,000	0.26%	0.13%
20	Belarus	10,000,000	20,000	0.20%	0.13%

According to Table 1, 90% of world Jewry is contained in only 6 countries (USA, Israel, France, Canada, UK and Russia). Today the world Jewish population is about 15 million, still less than the population of 1939.

The 20th century was the era of a great dispersion of Jews throughout the world. In 1910 the largest populations of Jews were in North America, Central Europe and Russia, Middle East, and North Africa.

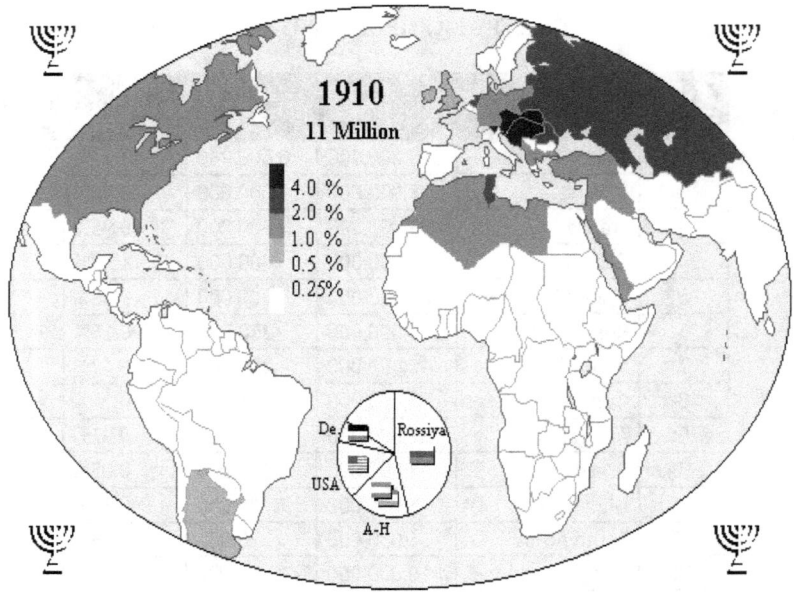

FIGURE 4

MAP OF THE WORLD JEWISH POPULATION IN 1910
(White 2003)

Three big events generated mass immigrations: the Bolshevik revolution (1917), the Holocaust (1933-1945), and the founding of the State of Israel (May 15, 1948). The world Jewish population in 1939 was about 17 million. After the Holocaust, in 1945 there were about 11 million Jews, the same population as in 1910. The European Jewish communities had been destroyed.

The next map shows the mass immigration of Jews from Central Europe; in 1939 there were more than 3 million Jews in Poland, the *American Jewish Yearbook* reports, and there are just 3,200 today. More than 4 million Jews lived in the Soviet Union. After the fall of the Berlin's Wall, 1.5 million immigrated in Israel, more than 1 million in the Americas and also about 1 million in Europe. Millions of Jews lived in Arabic regions of

North Africa and Middle East in 1910 until the founding of the State of Israel. I myself was born in Morocco. Thenceforward, a sequence of state approved expulsions made it difficult for Jews to live in Arabic countries. In 1995, the Middle East was almost empty of Jews except for Israel. The next map is clear and compared to the previous one does not need any comment.

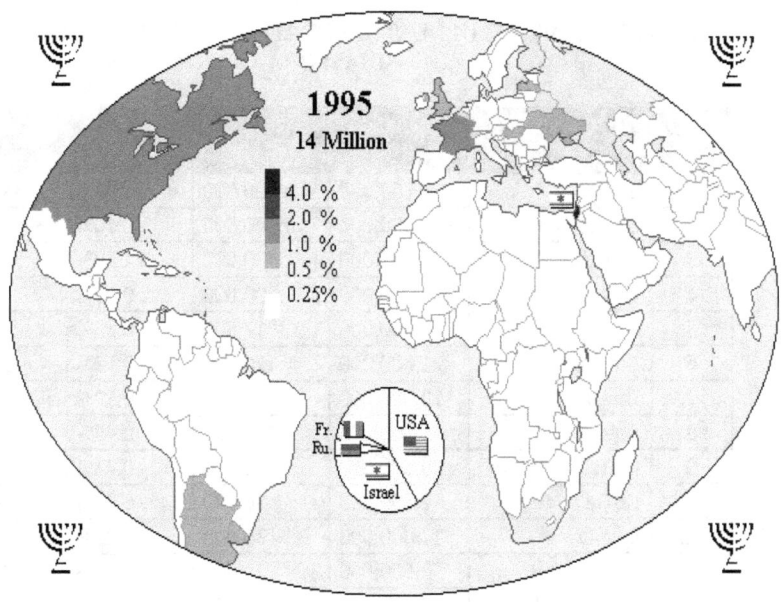

FIGURE 5

MAP OF THE WORLD JEWISH POPULATION IN 1995
(White 2003)

The Jewish diaspora predated Second World War by a thousand eight hundred years. However, the diaspora was reconfigured after the Holocaust. Today, only thirty countries have 10,000 Jews or more. But in addition there are seventy countries in the world that have a small population; between 100 and 9,999. I have not included these seventy countries in Tables 1 and 2. This information is available for these countries on the web site of the Jewish Virtual library.[1]

The 30 countries presented in the next Table have more than 15 million Jews, the remaining 200 thousand Jews are spread among the seventy other countries.

TABLE 2

WORLD'S JEWISH POPULATION SORTED BY PERCENTAGE IN THE DIASPORA

Rank	Country	Population	Jews	% in country	% of diaspora
1	Israel	7,500,000	6 000 000	76.00%	38.00%
2	United States	310,000,000	6,500,000	2.10%	43.33%
3	Canada	34,000,000	400,000	1.18%	2.67%
4	France	63,000,000	600,000	0.95%	4.00%
5	Uruguay	3,300,000	17,500	0.53%	0.12%
6	Australia	21,000,000	110,000	0.52%	0.73%
7	Hungary	10,000,000	50,000	0.50%	0.33%
8	Argentina	41,000,000	200,000	0.49%	1.33%
9	United Kingdom	63,000,000	300,000	0.48%	2.00%
10	Latvia	2,500,000	10,000	0.40%	0.07%
11	Belgium	11,000,000	35,000	0.32%	0.23%
12	Switzerland	7,600,000	20,000	0.26%	0.13%
13	Netherlands	17,000,000	40,000	0.24%	0.27%
14	Belarus	10,000,000	20,000	0.20%	0.13%
15	Russia	140,000,000	250,000	0.18%	1.67%
16	Ukraine	45,000,000	80,000	0.18%	0.53%
17	Sweden	9,500,000	15,000	0.16%	0.10%
18	South Africa	51,000,000	75,000	0.15%	0.50%
19	Chile	17,000,000	25,000	0.15%	0.17%
20	Germany	82,000,000	120,000	0.15%	0.80%
21	Brazil	195,000,000	100,000	0.05%	0.67%

---

[1] http://www.jewishvirtuallibrary.org/jsource/Judaism/jewpop.html (accessed on January 15, 2013).

Table 2 is important to show the impact of the Jewish population, which can be disguised by the raw numbers. There are less Jews in Israel than in the United States, but the Jewish people in Israel are 75% of the total population. The Jews in Canada, who are about equal to the number in England, form a larger percentage of Canada's smaller population. Thus, the Jewish presence in, for instance, Uruguay (where there is a Jewish Adventist congregation) where the Jewish population is less than twenty thousand people, is comparable percentage wise to England.

TABLE 3

LANGUAGES SPOKEN BY THE JEWISH POPULATION

Rank	Language	% In World	% In Diaspora
1.	English (US, U.K, Canada, S.A., Australia)	50.0	75.3
2.	Hebrew (Israel)	34.8	
3.	French (France)	4.0	6.2
4.	Spanish (South America, Mexico, Spain)	2.7	3.3
5.	Russian (Russia, Israel)	2.8	2.8
6.	Ukrainian (Ukraine)	1.4	4.0

90% of the world's Jewish population speaks English or Hebrew (USA, Israel, Canada, UK, Australia, South Africa). The languages with the next largest numbers are Hebrew and French (see Table 3).

The World Jewish Messianic Population

In the 1970s, when I first experienced the Messianic movement, it was still in its infancy. As I recounted in the first chapter, I was shocked by the way the Messianic Church in Paris I visited had given up the Sabbath and the Torah. That is why when I accepted Yeshua I joined the Seventh-day Adventist Church. To my understanding, it was the closest church to the Bible. Yet over time I have witnessed barriers to Jews becoming Seventh-day Adventists in spite of all the points in common that Jews and Adventists share. Thus was formed the problem I explore in this dissertation: for if the Seventh-day Adventist church was not succeeding in spreading the word of Yeshua in the Jewish community, then surely we needed a deep diagnosis of the structure of the Mission. The condition for a new mission strategy was an understanding of the historical background of Christian anti-Semitism, of which the Jewish community is well aware.

Of course, today there are hundreds of thousands of Jews who have accepted Yeshua in a worldwide Messianic movement. These "Messianic" Jews are joining all types of churches, some Messianic, but also Catholic, Protestant, Evangelical, and even Jehovah's Witnesses.

It is very difficult to know the exact number of Messianic Jews in the world. Most estimates give a range of 250,000 to 500,000 people. A reasonable number would be 350,000 according to Simon Dein, with 160,000 Messianic Jews living in the United States of America (45%) (2009, 80).

The Israeli Population

The last current report of the Israeli Central Bureau of Statistics (December, 2012) puts the Israeli population at 7,956,000. Some 6,000,000 people (75.40% of the population) are Jewish Israelis, 1,642,000 (20.6%) are Israeli Arabs, and those not identified as either make up the remaining 314,000 (4%)[2]. The Jewish population in Israel is divided by the Central Bureau of Statistics as listed in the Table 4 and 5:

---

[2] http://www1.cbs.gov.il/reader/?MIval=cw_usr_view_SHTML&ID=705 (accessed January 7, 2013).

TABLE 4

CULTURE, RELIGION, AND RACE IN ISRAEL

Culture/Religion/Race	Percent & Number
Jewish non-believers in Yeshua	70 % ± 5.3 Million
Christian Jews or Messianic Jews	5.5% ± 0.4 Million
Arab Muslims	15 % ± 1.148 Million
Arab Christians	5.5 % ± 0.4 Million
Foreign or unknown	4% ± 0.3 Million

TABLE 5

TYPES OF JEWS IN ISRAEL

Type of Jews	Percentage of all Jews
Ultra-orthodox	8%
Practicing Jews	12%
Traditional Religious Jews	13%
Traditional Jews	25%
Secular Jews	42%

My fieldwork was mainly among "traditional" or "secular" Jews, who make up 67% of the population, although I have also interviewed a few Orthodox Jews.

The Israeli Messianic Population

It is important to understand that citizenship in Israel is only given to Jews who do not believe in Yeshua. Thus, the Central Bureau of Statistics does not present statistics about Messianic or Christian Jews; nor does the state recognize them. It is estimated that there are about 15,000 Messianic Jews in Israel.

The best survey of the Messianic population was done in 1999 by the Caspari Center for Biblical and Jewish Studies. It was published by the United Christian Council in Israel (Kjær-Hansen and Skjott 1999).

According to this survey, there are about 5,000 people in Israel who can be described as Messianic Jews in a Messianic congregation. The survey did not count members of international congregations (except for the King of Kings Hebrew-speaking congregation) and other Christian denominations. The survey's definition of Messianic Jews, therefore, excluded Jews in other Christian denominations. Of these 5,000 people, 72% are adults and 28% are children. 61% are Jewish, 18% Non-Jewish but married to a Jew. 6% are non-Jewish Israelis, and 15% are non-Jewish non-Israelis (mostly foreign workers).

Since the collapse of the Soviet Union, a large influx of Russian Jews has increased the number of Messianic Jews. 42% of the Messianic Jews in the Survey are Russian speaking (Kjær-Hansen and Skjott 1999, 72). The survey covered seven Israeli districts:

TABLE 6

MESSIANIC DEMOGRAPHIC ACCORDING TO DISTRICT

Districts	Total	Adults	Children
District 1: Jerusalem	1,051	711	340
District 2: Northern Israel	754	531	223
District 3: Haifa	1,142	869	273
District 4: Central	633	438	195
District 5: Tel Aviv	836	623	213
District 6: Southern	421	292	129
District 7: Judea/Samaria	35	21	14

These statistics are from 1999. During the last eleven years, the Messianic movement has grown considerably. Even in 1999, according to the survey, not all Messianic congregations agreed to participate, making it likely there are more Messianic Jews outside of this count.

Very few Messianic Jews accept to reveal their membership of Christian churches and denominations. When Kjær-Hansen and Skjott asked how many attended international congregations, they listed very small numbers: Baptist Church (4), Christ Church (8), Mount Zion Fellowship (5), Redeemer Church (0), St Paul Church (0) and the Scottish Church (0), St Andrew's Church (1), Baptist Village Church (1) Immanuel Lutheran Church (5). The most successful international churches are the King of Kings Church (71), and the Narkis Street English Congregation (20) (Kjær-Hansen and Skjott 1999, 75).

Focus Group

My "Messianic" interviews were done through the only focus group I personally organized. I discovered that people were very reluctant to meet together and share about their faith in Yeshua.

My focus group was composed of six people who had accepted Yeshua: Samuel, Sarah, Lea, Isaac, Salomon, and Rachel[3]. Two of them, Samuel and Salomon, are Sabra, that is, born in Israel. No member was from an Orthodox family, but Samuel and Salomon came from a traditional Jewish family, even though they later became secular Jews. Four were born in the former Soviet Union and had immigrated to Israel in the 1990. They attributed their secular beliefs to communism and Soviet era anti-Semitism. The common factor uniting the group's conversion stories was how instrumental close

---

[3] Even though I have used Jewish first names they are pseudonyms, not their real name.

friends were. Samuel and Salomon had been converted by their wives, and the others discovered Yeshua from friends at work or school.

Most said that they accepted Yeshua in a relatively short period of time: Samuel and Sarah after three months, Isaac and Lea after six months, and Rachel after approximately one year. Salomon, however, took many years to accept Yeshua.

My findings through the focus group are summarized on Table 17 in the appendix D. Here I list, in brief, what attracted them: (1) Samuel: quotations of Hebrew Scriptures in the New Testament, Yeshua as Messiah of Israel being presented as a Jew and Yeshua's love in the New Testament. (2) Sarah: She already believed in God, the example of her own family and the testimony of friends. (3) Lea: She had for long time an intuition regarding a great conflict between good and evil, She also was sure about the existence of a Savior, her Bible reading helped her discover Yeshua. (4) Isaac: His reading of the New Testament, the description of Yeshua in the New Testament and the expression of Yeshua's love for the Hebrew Scriptures. (5) Rachel: Her reading of the Bible and the New Testament, Yeshua' teaching and deeds and her personal conviction. (6) Salomon: The example of his wife, and a direct revelation from God.

The hindrances were as follows:

1. Samuel: some Christian doctrines such as the triune God, and the opposition of his family.

2. Sarah: She had no hindrances or obstacles, accepting Yeshua was easy for her.

3. Lea: The main obstacle for Lea was her Muslim husband.

4. Isaac: The main hindrance for him was his family, and in particular the opposition of his wife, which resulted in their divorce.

5. Rachel: The main obstacle was her father who was against her research about Yeshua.

6. Salomon: his hindrances were his personal prejudices, especially the fact that Christians have persecuted Jews, his family, and some Christian doctrines.

From this list, we can see that reading the Bible is the greatest path to conversion, and—derivative from this—the discovery of the Jewish of Yeshua, while the main hindrances came from the resistance of their own families and, secondarily for some, certain Christian doctrines.

Interviews

Interviewing was far easier than organizing focus groups because the people were contacted individually. One on one, they were less cautious. Because of the sensitivity of the subject, especially in the country (Israel) where the interviews took place, I chose to disguise the names of those interviewed to secure their privacy. I interviewed the following people:

1. Moshe was born in a traditional Jewish family in which no great stress was laid on observing the Mosaic Law rigidly. He converted to Orthodox and then to Lubavitcher Judaism.

2. Yaacov is a traditional Orthodox rabbi, who ministered in France for many years until he, immigrated to Israel in the 1990s, where he continued his pastoral work in Jerusalem. He has written many books, including one called *Chalom Jesus* (Grunewald 2000).

3. Manashe is an orthodox migrant from the United States. He is a very convinced Jew, and is a member of an anti-missionary organization. I have included his interview because his point of view is interesting and very insightful.

4. Michael, who is an observant, traditional Jew. He is a dentist in Jerusalem. He married the daughter of a great rabbi and has a very open mind.

5. Shimon was born in Europe during the Holocaust, and lost his family and both parents. He is secular in outlook. His experiences were so traumatic that when he married a Jewish lady and they gave birth to a daughter he did not want to reveal to her that they were Jews until her seventeenth birthday. Today, the family lives in Jerusalem, where they are proudly Israeli. He respects all religions, but does not practice Judaism in any strict way, even though he goes to the synagogue from time to time.

6. Ruth was born in Israel and went to the United States to complete her studies to become a Rabbi in the Liberal Jewish community. She now works in Israel as a Rabbi of a Liberal congregation. The results of the interviews are listed on Table 18, Appendix D.

Conclusion: I interviewed Jews from different sectors of the Jewish community. In the next section, I summarized their attractions to Yeshua and hindrances to accepting him. The most resistance to Yeshua is, predictably, around those with the most Orthodox attitude.

TABLE 7

REACTIONS TOWARDS YESHUA

Orthodox Jews $\Rightarrow$	Very Hostile to Yeshua
Traditional Jews $\Rightarrow$	Indifferent to Yeshua
Secular Jews $\Rightarrow$	Don't know Yeshua
Liberal Jews $\Rightarrow$	Could accept him as Prophet

Participant Observations

I was involved as a participant observer in three different milieus: at a Jewish synagogue in Ashdod (south of Tel Aviv), at a Messianic worship service in Jerusalem and at an Adventist synagogue in Jerusalem. Table 19 in Appendix D gives a summary of my motives, notes and inferences. What I have discovered is that the synagogues are investing a lot of money to make their building and sanctuary attractive and beautiful, when the Messianic congregation I visited in Jerusalem was not so attractive and rather old fashioned, and the SDA congregation was not Jewish in its rituals or orientation at all, that means not attractive to Jews too.

Secondary Data

I wanted to include in this dissertation some secondary data drawn from my literature review. The first one is a survey conducted by the organization Jews for Jesus, and the second one is composed of stories of Jewish conversion to Messianic or Christian denominations.

Jews for Jesus' Survey

The Jews for Jesus ministry in Israel surveyed the Jewish population to ascertain their understanding of Yeshua (see Appendix C). They contacted a professional company to carry out the research, but after some time elapsed, the company reported back that their employees were intimidated and insulted by the people they were interviewing. After a few weeks, the company offered to refund the money, as they couldn't perform the work. However, Jews for Jesus found a solution, sending members along who were familiar with the community to accompany the survey takers. The company agreed, completed the survey after one month.

Summary of Attractions: 80% know the name of the Messiah (72% Yeshu and 8% Yeshua). However, only 10% of the population consider him to be a Jew. When Jews first read the New Testament they are often surprised to discover that Yeshua was a Jew and that he is presented as a Jewish Messiah. The misperception of Yeshua by the majority of the Jewish population is a major challenge to our mission. A majority (62%)

knows that he performed great miracles, and a lesser majority are most impressed by the miracle of Yeshua walking on the water (59%). Only 21% of the population takes a positive perception of Yeshua, while 6% labeled him a prophet, and 5% labeled him the Jewish Messiah.

In contrast to the 21% who took a positive view of Yeshua, 40% viewed Yeshua's message positively. They used words such as brotherly love, compassion, peace, humility, forgiveness, patience, and salvation to describe it. Thirty-one percent of those interviewed agree that Yeshua's message is about "atonement." According to the survey, a third of the population has a positive or correct perception of Yeshua' ministry and message.

Summary of Hindrances: Most of the Jewish population calls Yeshua "Yeshu," not "Yeshua." Yeshu is an acronym of ימח שום וזרכו meaning "May his name and memory be deleted." However, only 2% knew this meaning.

The third question shows us that only around 11% of the Hebrew speaking Jews in Israel link the name Yeshua to its meaning, "salvation." In fact, the majority confused "Yeshua" with "Joshua," the successor of Moses (62%).

Conclusion: This survey illuminates the landscape of partial knowledge or ignorance concerning Yeshua. 80% have heard about him, and 62% have heard about his miracles, but there is little knowledge of Yeshua's Jewish context. It is even surprising to the Jewish population that Yeshua was a Jew and proclaimed his mission as the Jewish Messiah.

Jewish Conversion in Literature

I have included many of the case studies in Schoeman (2003), which present histories of Jews who have accepted Yeshua and have joined Messianic organizations. But also include histories of those who joined regular Christian denominations (Catholics

Lutherans, Calvinist, and so on). I have used these histories to shed some further light on the topic of this dissertation.

Jews Converted to Catholicism

Jews who convert to Christianity (see appendix D, Table 20) often try to find the roots of their faith in their new Christian beliefs. This tendency is experienced by Jews even when they enter a church such as the Catholic Church. Rasolind Moss once, paradoxically, said, "becoming Catholic is 'the most Jewish thing a person can do'" (Schoeman 2003, 323). Schoeman also mentions the conversion story of the French Cardinal of Paris, Jean-Marie (Aaron) Lustiger:

> I explained [to my father] that baptism would not make me abandon my Jewish condition—quite the contrary. It would lead me to find it, to receive the plenitude of its meaning. I did not have the feeling that I was betraying my heritage, or camouflaging myself or abandoning anything whatsoever. Just the opposite: I felt that I was going to find the import, the meaning of what I had received at birth.
>
> [My instruction prior to baptism] confirmed my keen intuition that Christianity is the continuation of Judaism. . . . Christianity is the fruit of Judaism! To be specific: I believe in Christ, the Messiah of Israel. Something that I had carried within me for years, without having spoken about it to anyone, crystallized. I knew that Judaism held the hope of the Messiah. I knew that the response to the scandal of suffering of God's promises to his people. And I knew that Jesus is the Messiah, the Christ of God...
>
> Until the Messiah's coming in glory, the Jew remains, and he remains a Jew, whether he is Christian or not (Schoeman 2003, 323-326).

Schoeman also cites the case of the Lemann brothers converted to Catholicism in the 19th century, when they were very young. They became prominent priests working closely with Pope Pius IX. About their origin they said: "A Jew in becoming Catholic does not change his religion, but fulfills his religion, completes it, crowns it. The Jew became Catholic is the religious man par excellence, who has grown into his fullness, as the seed grows into the flower" (2003, 326).

Schoeman tells the story of the conversion of Alphonse Ratisbonne, a French Jewish Banker who followed in the footsteps of his older brother, who became a priest. Alphonse claimed that he was granted an extraordinary vision of the Virgin Mary that determined his conversion:

> I had only been in the church a moment when I was suddenly seized with an indescribable agitation of mind. I looked up and found that the rest of the building had disappeared. One single chapel seemed to have gathered all the light and concentrated it in itself. In the midst of this radiance I saw someone standing on the altar, a lofty shinning figure, all majesty and sweetness, the Virgin Mary just as she looks on the medal. Some irresistible force drew me towards her. She motioned to me to kneel down and when I did so, she seemed to approve. Though she never said a word. I understood her perfectly (2003, 331).

Another fascinating story is told by Rabbi Zollin, the Great Rabbi of Rome. While performing the Yom Kippur service in his synagogue, he saw Jesus:

> It was the Day of Atonement in the fall of 1944, and I was presiding over the religious service in the Temple. The day was nearing its end, and I was all-alone in the midst of a great number of persons. I began to feel as though a fog were creeping in my soul; it became denser, and I wholly lost touch with the men and things around me. . . . And just then I saw with my mind's eye a meadow sweeping upward, with bright grass,.,.,.,. In this meadow I saw Jesus Christ clad in a white mantle, and beyond His head the blue sky. I experienced the greatest interior peace. (2003, 337-338)

It is interesting to notice that Rabbi Zollin did not feel that he was leaving or betraying Judaism. When people asked Zollin why he had given up the synagogue he answered, "But I have not given it up. Christianity is the integration, completion or crown of the Synagogue. For the Synagogue was a promise, and Christianity is the fulfillment of that promise" (Schoeman 2003, 341).

Schoeman's last example is of Charles Rich, who was born in a devout Hasidic family in a small village in Hungary. He immigrated with his family to New York and lost his faith. One day while passing by a Catholic church, he entered it. He described what happened inside this way, "All of a sudden something flashed through my mind and I heard these words spoken in it, 'Of course it is true, Christ is God, is God come down to make Himself visible in the flesh. The words of the Gospels are true, literally true'" (2003, 343).

Jews Who Converted to Evangelical, Protestant or Messianic Churches

On the Protestant or evangelical side we have some related experiences in a book edited by Ruth Rosen (1992). It contains fifteen conversion stories (see Appendix D Table 21). I pulled the following themes of attraction from these accounts:

- The quest for spirituality
- The prayer experience.
- The feeling that one has fallen, or is unholy, and the need for salvation, which Jesus fulfills.
- God answering prayers of other Christians.
- Reading the Bible, the New Testament, the Jewish Siddur and Messianic magazines.
- Discovering the Messianic prophecies and accepting the sacrifice of the Messiah.
- Discovering the Jewishness of Jesus.
- Contextualization and use of Hebrew words as Messiah instead of Christ.
- Discovering that Yeshua was the way he talked.
- Discovering the Jewish Roots of Christianity.
- Attending Christian school
- Meeting other Messianic Jews.
- Talk with a rabbi. Attending small groups of religious minded individuals.
- Act of kindness and genuine love from other Christians and pastors.
- Discovering possible intimacy with God and Jesus touching their heart.
- Extraordinary vision of Jesus.
- The Christian faith of spouses and the testimony of other members of their family.
- Reading a Jews for Jesus' pamphlet
- Jesus' portrait in the movie "*Quo-Vadis*".

- Christmas carols.

Their hindrances were:

- Opposition of Husband, family members, friends, bosses and even the Jewish community and Rabbis.
- Their old lifestyle and addictions to alcohol and other drugs.
- Prosperity and success.
- Personal prejudices against the Christian church its idolatry (Jesus' images).
- Christian doctrines (triune God).
- The fear of losing their Jewish identity.
- Anti-Semitism, the Holocaust, God's responsibilities, and in some cases memories of internment at Nazi camps.
- Need of strong evidence that Yeshua is the Messiah,

Analyzing my Data

The survey, interviews, focus groups, case studies, and other observations I gathered were transcribed into my computer. I used my own coding system, devised to label properties of the conversion process, according to the categories I am using in my Tables. My coding was very simple, that is, A1, A2, A3, A4, and so on, for attractions to Jesus, and H1, H2, H3, H4, and so on, for hindrances. From this I built the Tables summarizing what was previously presented.

Findings as a Result of this Research

Attractions: Through my interviews and readings I gathered 87 responses of things that attracted Jews to Jesus. Three of them were overwhelmingly more important than the other factors. The three are: Bible reading, discovering the Jewishness of Jesus, and the influence of friends and family members.

TABLE 8

ATTRACTIONS CLASSIFIED BY PRIORITY

35.5%	Reading the Bible
19.5%	Jewishness of Jesus
14%	Witness by Friends or family
8%	Direct revelation from God
7%	Search for Spirituality
7%	Reading a pamphlet or book
6%	Small group Ministry
2%	Talking with a Rabbi
1%	Used of Contextualized vocabulary

It is evident that the Bible is the most common gateway for Jews to encounter Yeshua (35.5%). This speaks to the most helpful thing a Christian can do to perform the mission among the Jews: offer a Bible or a version of the Apostolic Writings. Most of the people I met in my fieldwork had read the Bible or the Apostolic Writings. Surprisingly, although scholars often label Matthew as the most Jewish gospel, my own observation is that the gospel of John has the greatest impact. A theme that emerges from these accounts of Bible reading is the understanding of Yeshua through the prism of the Messianic prophecies. The suffering servant in Isaiah 53, and the seventy weeks in Daniel 9, have the most powerful effect. The later passage gives the exact date of the coming of the Messiah, and make clear that his death must occur before the destruction of Jerusalem.[4]

When Jews read the New Testament they discover that Yeshua was also a Jew. It surprises most of them. This is the second highest factor that attracts Jews to Jesus (19.5%). Many of these people were aware of the Christian Jesus, but are surprised by the

---

[4] Isaiah 53 includes this often cited sentence: "Surely he took up our infirmities and carried our sorrows, yet we considered him stricken by God, smitten by him, and afflicted. But he was pierced for our transgressions, he was crushed for our iniquities; the punishment that brought us peace was upon him, and by his wounds we are healed" (53:4-5). Dan 9:24-27 says "And after threescore and two weeks shall Messiah be cut off, but not for himself: and the people of the prince that shall come shall destroy the city and the sanctuary; and the end thereof shall be with a flood, and unto the end of the war desolations are determined" (9:26).

clearly Jewish Yeshua of the Apostolic Writings. His love, his work for the poor, his interest in widows and orphans also attract Jews to him.

In the life of every Jew who has accepted Yeshua, there is usually an encounter with friends, family members or even a pastor (14% of the people studied found their witnessing attractive). In my set of conversion stories, God often sends someone to help the potential convert understand that Yeshua is the Messiah. Most testimonies point to lay people (wives, work friends, neighbors, and so on).

Another important factor in conversion is a pre-existing interest in personal spiritual research (8%). There were also people who received a vision of Jesus or heard a voice telling them the way of salvation (7%).

Being prayed for plays a significant role in these testimonies. Several converts mentioned their feeling of a link between someone praying for them and their discovery of Yeshua.

Another important factor is attending a small group ministry or a church service. Some were attracted by the liturgy, others by the fact that the church was not a place of idolatry, with no statues or images.

The use of a contextualized vocabulary did not register as an important factor: it received a rating of one percent in the matrix of conversion factors. This may be due to the relative absence of the contextualized mission in Israel until recently.

Hindrances: I gathered 45 references to various hindrances to conversion the most important are listed in the Table 9.

Family opposition is the greatest hindrance (45%). The bonds of community among Jews are such that conversion to Yeshua is often interpreted as betrayal of the community. Being Jewish means belonging to a special culture, people, and history. When a convert accepts Yeshua, his or her family will often say, "You are not a Jew anymore." This happened to me.

TABLE 9

HINDRANCES CLASSIFIED BY PRIORITY

46%	Family opposition
11%	Fear of giving up one's Jewish identity
9%	Christian doctrines (Trinity)
9%	No Hindrances
9%	Anti-Semitism
7%	Prejudices
7%	Lifestyle (businessman, alcohol…)
2%	Need scientific evidences

A second closely linked factor is the fear of losing one's identity (11%). Jewish identity has developed over the past 4,000 years. It includes persecution of the worst kind, culminating in surviving one of the great mass murders in history. Against this persecution, Jews developed a proud identity that literally helped them survive. David Chansky was even tempted to go back to Judaism because of his sense of identity loss. "However, part of the reason I was susceptible to doubting my faith in Jesus was that it seemed to preclude my Jewish identity" (Rosen 1992, 291). It was only when Chansky found a Messianic congregation realized the Jewishness of Yeshua that his doubts were healed.

> When, in more recent years, I became aware of the fact that Yeshua never rejected his Jewishness….I realized there was no need for me to forsake those things, which the Messiah himself affirmed. The joy of my identity as a Jew was restored, as there was finally a coming together of my Jewishness and faith in Jesus (295).

It is understandable that some who begin a journey towards Yeshua are afraid of losing their Jewish identity, or of no longer being recognized as Jews by their family members or friends. This is especially the case in Israel, where the Government does not recognize Messianic Jews, and helps to explain why most of the Messianic Jews who emigrate to Israel do not reveal their belief in Yeshua.

Another important hindrance is a doctrinal one. A small percentage of Jews fear that believing in the Christian doctrine of the Trinity makes them idolaters (9%). As a physician in Jerusalem said to my wife, there are only two religions—Judaism and Islam. All others are idolatrous. Some Jews have been taught that it is a sin to enter a church. As Michael said to me, a Jew may enter a mosque to pray, but not a church.

Most of my interviewees don't understand how Christians can have "three gods." Vera Schlamm accepted the invitation of a Baptist pastor to visit his church. She reports: "Still, as I walked into church with them, I recited the Shema. Like many Jewish people, I thought Christians worshipped three gods and I wanted God to know that I believed in him alone" (Rosen 1992, 149).

The long history of Jewish persecution by the church repels many Jews (9%). Vera Schlamm and Laura Wertheim are typical examples of this feeling. Vera was thinking about accepting Jesus, but after speaking with a Baptist Pastor she said, "I felt, how can I go into enemy territory? After all, the people who persecuted me were Christians as far as I was concerned. I certainly didn't want to be a Christian. I just wanted to be right with God" (Rosen 1992, 150). Vera is a Holocaust survivor. We can understand her sense that conversion is betrayal. By accepting Jesus she wants "to be right with God", but she still does not want to be a Christian.

Laura lived in Germany during WWII. She was with her family in the concentration camp and vowed she "would never forget the murder of her grandparents or the fact that they were killed because they were Jews" (1992, 243).

I was surprised at the tenacity of old myths. An Orthodox Jew told me the legend about the bastard Jesus and about how he performed miracles thanks to being branded with the name of God. I, too, heard such stories as a child, but find it astonishing that adults would continue to believe them.

The second surprise was to see how varied were the beliefs in Israel's Jewish community. My research constantly pushed me up against the fact that even within each branch of Judaism there are a wide variety of beliefs. I found it fascinating to understand my interviewees thoughts about Jesus and Christianity. Recently I was on a bus in Jerusalem and spoke with a religious man, who told me that in God's eyes Jews may be religious, secular, liberal, or whatever they want, since for God they are all Jews, all people of Israel. This is close to how the community explains itself.

The third surprise was to find an open minded attitude towards Yeshua. The topic of this research was not what Jews thought about Christianity, or Paul, or Peter, but Yeshua. My interviewees may be upset with Christianity and its history. They often blamed Paul for provoking the divisions between Jews and Christians, but never Yeshua, whose life and actions were admired.

My fourth surprise was that the way to Yeshua was so often facilitated by a special intermediary, a person who the spiritual pilgrim already knows. Moishe and Ceil Rosen (founders of Jews for Jesus) have discovered this as well. In their book on the mission to the Jews, they report: "Though the details vary, a common thread runs through these stories. All of them, even those that contain supernatural experiences, show how God used people who already knew Him to help bring unbelievers to saving faith in Jesus. A few were professional ministers, but many were ordinary lay Christians—like you" (Rosen and Rosen 1998, 44).

Another surprise was to discover that Jews don't generally care about Christian theology or Christian lifestyles. It is not that Jews are ready to accept doctrines such as the Trinity, or the Messiahship of Yeshua, but they definitely are positive about Yeshua, separate him from the Church, and understand him in an admiring way. Christian theology contributes less to conversion than the incarnation of Yeshua, the Holy Spirit, and the reading of the Apostolic Writings.

Discovered Research Gaps

At the beginning of my research I hypothesized that theological concepts such as supersessionism (replacement theology) were primary obstacles for Jews. This was not borne out in my interviews and survey. Among the Jews I contacted, Jesus and Christian history are clearly held apart. This is good news, and speaks to the way we can refocus mission strategy on Yeshua's life and works, instead of the church that supposedly represents him. However, I am not claiming to give a complete picture of Yeshua's image in the entire Jewish community.

Summary

Putting the themes of my dissertation, "Attractions and Hindrances in the Proclamation of the Gospel to Jews", in the context of my ministry, I can clearly see that among them, the reputation of Yeshua is in contrast to Christianity and the Church. Many Rabbis and philosophers (Buber, Lapide, Klausner) have claimed (or reclaimed) Yeshua as a Jew. At the same time, Christianity or the Church is still often considered pagan and polytheistic.

Jews are very sensitive about the anti-Semitic history of the Christian Church. Recently when the Pope decided to beatify Pope Pius XII, the pope during the World War II, Jewish people all over the world protested, claiming that Pius XII was, at best, tepid in his defense of the Jews against the Nazis. It is very common on Jewish websites or in Jewish newspapers to see articles about what the Church has done to Jewish people throughout history, listing all the pogroms and persecution, and so on. Yet Yeshua is seen with much more fellow feeling. A Jew who lives in Israel has written a book about Jesus in which he says the following:

> Jesus of Nazareth lived. He continues to live, not only in the church that rests on him—or, more precisely, in the many churches and denominations that claim him—but also in his Jewish people, whose martyrdom he embodies, is not the suffering Jesus, the Jesus scorned as he

hangs dying on the cross, a likeness for his entire people who, tortured and bloodied, have been hanged time and again on the cross of anti-Semitism? And is the Easter message of the resurrection not a parable for postwar Israel, which has risen out of the abasement and disgrace of the darkest twelve years in its history to a new incarnation? (Ben Chorin 2001, 19).

This quotation could have been written by a Christian. There are more and more Jewish scholars today who respect Jesus, his ministry, and his teaching.

The respect for Yeshua is, however, affected by the school of Christian critics of the New Testament (historico-critical reading of the Bible) who question the basis of the gospels. In my literature review, I read some Jewish scholars who quote Christians who do not believe what is written in the New Testament.

David Flusser provides an example of this Christian behavior that is reported by Brad Young in his book about Jesus. He gives this testimony,

> David Flusser, an Orthodox Jew who teaches at the Hebrew University, has often related a true experience, which shocked him. He was lecturing in Germany before a group of Protestant theologians, some of whom served as pastors. He described his work as a New Testament scholar researching the life and teachings of Jesus in Israel at the Hebrew University. Flusser remarked that through a careful method of linguistic analysis and comparative study, the actual words of Jesus could be heard and understood.
> One theologian present completely rejected Flusser's comments. He explained before the learned servants of the church that he had actually studied with Rudolf Bultmann himself. The degree of reverence and awe which are accorded to Rudolf Bultmann in theological settings such as this must be appreciated to fully understand this story. The room was hushed with revered silence.
> The theologian continued with a polite way of telling the professor from Israel that he was absolutely mistaken. The words of Jesus are forever lost. No one can hear the voice of Jesus today. In fact, in his intensive studies with Bultmann they discovered that only one verse in the Gospels comes from Jesus.
> Flusser was interested in this active exchange and scholarly interaction. The reference to one verse aroused his curiosity. Flusser asked the question, "Which verse actually goes back to Jesus?" The theologian replied, "I forgot" (1995, 255).

Christian skepticism can only take Jews away from Yeshua. If Christians are not able to believe what is written in their Bible, how can they expect other people to? Fortunately, such attitudes are not widespread among common believers. A parallel skepticism about the Bible exists in Judaism among Reform and Liberal Jews. Orthodox and traditional Jews believe and trust in their Scripture.

This research set out to understand attractions and hindrances in the proclamation of the gospel to Jews. Using surveys, interviews, and previous literature on this subject, I was able to tabulate and code both categories

The attractions and hindrances are relative to the kind of Jew who is receiving the message. Ultra-Orthodox Jews are very closed to the idea of Jesus being the Messiah, while many Liberal Jews are open and accepting of Jesus. The latter are not, however, enthusiastic about Christianity, which is why they keep their distance from the Church.

Among Orthodox Jews, there are other messianic cults, such as those of Rabbi Schnersshon or Rabbi Nachman Mi-Braslev. These groups are usually very strongly opposed to accepting Yeshua. Some of these groups have founded an anti-missionary organization—*Yad Leachim*—which works against all Messianic congregations in Israel.

I have encountered many other Jews who interpret Yeshua as a man who wanted to do wonderful things and reform the corrupted Jewish leadership of his time. In my experience, many myths and misunderstanding about Yeshua are still current in the Jewish community. Much of this stems from views of the Catholic Church, which is often viewed as an anti-Semitic Church that would be happy to see the destruction of the Jewish people. The inquisition, the pogroms, and the cooperation of certain priests and church officials with the Nazis in WWII has constructed a very thick barrier to conversion to belief in Yeshua, and elicits hostility to Christian missionaries who try to convert Jews. Some in the Jewish community even equate mission work with ipso facto anti-Semitisms. Jews believe that the point of Jewish evangelism is to dissolve and assimilate the Jewish community. And it is true that, historically, this is what Christian churches have advocated.

For these reasons, Jews still react very radically towards other Jews who have accepted Jesus, interpreting conversion as going over to the 'enemy'. Legally, Israel refuses to extend return status to converted Jews, as all other Jews are. The so-called "law of return" is clear in Israel. Any person who can prove that one of his/her parents or his/her grandparents is a Jew has the right to immigrate and claim Israeli citizenship. This citizenship is granted to everyone, religious, secular, atheist, Zionist, anti-Zionist, and so on, but it is systematically refused to Jews who have accepted Jesus[5]. The rationale is that Jews who have accepted Jesus will operate as missionaries in the country.

Modern Jews oppose Christian and Messianic theology and have developed their own theological arguments. They interpret all the "Messianic prophecies" in a way that denies that Jesus could have fulfilled them. They read the Apostolic Writings critically, accuse Paul of founding a Gentile *Goy* religion completely separated from Judaism, reject Christian doctrines such as the trinity, and deny that a death of a human being (Jesus' death) could be for the salvation of others

In my research, this counter-movement has had little effect on Messianic Jews." Manashe, my Orthodox interviewee, believed that "after studying the Bible Jews who are Messianic return to Judaism." My research does not support this claim at all.

Instead, Jews who had read the Apostolic Writings and found out about Yeshua were very much attracted by his personality, his ministry of love, his preaching rooted in Judaism, and his practice of Judaism. He was born as a Jew and died as a Jew. When they do a comparative study of the Old and New Testament and especially the so-called

---

[5] The sections 4A and 4B of the Law of Return, 5710-1950 speak about the relatives and family members of those who can immigrate to Israel and it is specified "except for a person who has been a Jew and has voluntarily changed his religion". This law was voted on March 10, 1970 (Sefer Ha-Chukkim of 5712, p. 146; LSI vol. VI, p. 50)

Messianic Prophecies, I can testify that many are convinced that Jesus is the Messiah (especially Isa 53 and Dan 9, see note 4 page 61).

It is this course, which, I think, makes the presentation of the gospel to the Jews bear fruit. A careful presentation of such prophecies must be included.

My interviews and research among Jews who had accepted Yeshua were very encouraging and delightful. I am convinced that Yeshua can be preached to the Jews. Perhaps we have to be more proactive in order to touch those who have been called by God to know him.

CHAPTER 5

ATTRACTIONS AND HINDRANCES IN LITERATURE

The first section of this literature review presents two research questions and the definition of words used in this paper. In the second section I survey the relevant Jewish and Messianic (Christian) books from which it is possible to extract attractions and hindrances (theological, historical and sociological) to the mission to Israel's Jews. Jews throughout history have generally refused to accept Yeshua. In modern times, a number of Jews have become secularized, but relatively few have become Christian. Not surprisingly, I find more hindrances than attractions in the literature.

Attractions

In reading Jewish scholars' works on Yeshua for this literature review I discovered that there are some very interesting statements about Yeshua, his teaching, and his ministry. The suffering of the Jewish people at the hands of the church has been so traumatic that one might expect the blame to be put on Yeshua. On the contrary, Yeshua is still the great attraction. Still, there are more hindrances than attractions.

Respect for Yeshua's Life and Message

Before enumerating the most significant attractions, I want to quote an overview about the contemporary Jewish perspective on the person of Yeshua by Rabbi Michael J. Cook:

> Jesus was a Jew, and so were his followers…Jesus behaved as a Jew…Jesus was a great teacher of Jewish ethics…Jesus should be viewed against the Jewish context of his day, not in isolation…Such an approach

reveals that Jesus' uniqueness may have resided more with his personality than with his originality...Jesus may have deemed himself the Messiah, but, if so, he was mistaken; he did not bring about what was expected of the Jewish Messiah... The charges on which Jesus was arrested were political in orientation. Possibly his preaching of the coming of the kingdom of God was constructed as predicting or urging the overthrow of the Roman establishment along with its appointees (Cook 2001, 23-24).

Jewishness of Yeshua

The literature review shows a growing trend to reclaim Yeshua as a Jew. Today scholars agree that Jesus was born as a Jew and died as a Jew, and his teaching was Jewish and Pharisaic. This truth was pithily expressed by John Paul II in his visit in Mainz. He said, "To meet Jesus Christ is to meet Judaism" (Lapide 1981, 140). This is an enormous move by the Church; it corresponds to the "reclaiming of Yeshua" by Jewish scholars.

Jacob Klausner's 1925 *Jesus of Nazareth* marks a turning point in the Jewish interpretation of Jesus. Klausner builds on his nineteenth century and early 20th century forerunners, notably C. G. Montefiore, but these forebears were more concerned, in the liberal and reformed tradition, to make Jesus a universal figure, a sage like Buddha, whereas Klausner saw him as being uniquely Jewish in his roots and approach. Klausner makes the following conclusions about Jesus' knowledge:

> Jesus derived his entire knowledge and point of view from the Scriptures and from a few, at most, of the Palestinian apocryphal and pseudepigraphical writings and from the Palestinian Haggada and Midrash in the primitive form in which they were then current among the Jews (1989, 363).

Yeshua was a real Jew, and should be so presented by Christian missionaries. Klausner points out, "There were many Gentiles in Galilee, but Jesus was in no way influenced by them." Later he added, "Jesus spoke Aramaic and there is no hint that he knew Greek—none of his sayings shows any clear mark of Greek literary influence" (1989, 363).

Klausner was a precursor, he allowed other Jewish thinkers to have a vey positive view of Jesus. Martin Buber describes his relationship to Jesus in this way:

> For almost fifty years the New Testament has been one of my principal topics of study and I consider myself to be a good reader who listens without prejudice.... From my youth, I felt that Jesus was like a big brother to me. That Christianity considered Jesus as God and Redeemer was always apparent to me as a fact to take extremely seriously, one that I had to seek to understand for myself. That wish to understand resulted in my personal relationship with and a brotherly attitude towards Jesus, which only reinforced and purified me while I see Jesus in a stronger and purer light than ever (1991, 33).

Buber was one of the greatest Jewish philosophers of the 20th century; he was also practically active in Jewish-Christian relationships. His influence is mirrored in, for instance, the speeches of Pope John Paul II in his addresses to the Jewish community in Mainz on November 17, 1980 and in Jerusalem on March 26, 2000 (Henrix 2008, 67).

The turn to the Jewish Jesus has had a vast effect on scholarship concerning the historical Christ. Pinchas Lapide, an Orthodox Jew, developed a view of the evolution of the discovery of the Jewishness of Yeshua that aptly summarizes the discovery of Yeshua in contemporary Judaism:

> Lapide proposed, in 1976, four stages in the modern Jewish quest to recover the Jewish Jesus or "fifth Jesus." The first stage is characterized by those who highlight that which separates Jesus from Judaism by seeking out the non-Jewish elements of his teaching. The second is distinguished by those who highlight the commonalities between Jesus and the normative Judaism of his time, and dismiss all supposed non-Jewish elements of his teaching as anachronisms in the New Testament. Those who paint him as a rebel with regard not only to the Roman authorities but also the Sadducean establishment typify the third stage. The fourth stage is most accurately represented by those who understand Jesus' relationship to Judaism as a creative mix of contrast and harmony; both parts of which arise from within the boundaries of the normative Judaism of his day. Although Lapide's own research contains elements of

the second and third stages, particularly in its earliest incarnations, it is consistently most at home in the fourth (Galarneau 2009, 116).

A pertinent question brings this into focus: if Yeshua were living on earth today, where he would be more comfortable, in a church or in a synagogue? Surely it would be the latter. As Herbert Bronstein puts it, Yeshua would understand a "Reform Jewish synagogue" or even in "an Orthodox Jewish synagogue. He would at least understand the Hebrew language of prayers....Jesus would recognize various phraseologies of the prayers and would be at home with much of the content, metaphors, and ethos of synagogue prayer as it exists today" (Bronstein 2001, 45). This scholar shows that the prayers of Jesus were close to the prayers found in the Jewish tradition. The Lord's Prayer resembles the *Kaddish* (2001, 51), while the Beatitudes clearly reference Psalm 84:5, Psalm 1 and 2, or Psalm 119:1-2 (2001, 52). "The Old Testament and post-biblical literature contain a large number of Beatitudes, presenting them in a wide variety of forms and functions" (2001, 52).

As this brief survey of the literature shows, the resistance and objections to Yeshua that were common in medieval and early modern Judaism—for instance, in Maimonides—have generally disappeared in the more sophisticated circles of contemporary Judaic thought. If Yeshua's messianic mission is not embraced, it is, at least, sympathetically understood. As Bronstein writes: "I believe I could "talk Torah" with Jesus almost as easily as I could with my own spiritual ancestors, the Pharisees" (2001, 49).

The New Testament

The New Testament plays a special role in the rediscovery of the Jewish Yeshua. After all, the New Testament was written by Jews, and is a valid historical depiction of Second Temple Jewish life. Hidden by the accretions of the second and third century Christian interpretation that attempted to divorce Christianity from Judaism, the New

Testament became accessible to Jews in the 19th and 20th century as the Hellenic Christian interpretations were discredited.

> The tradition of the Gospel is first of all, in every respect simply a part of the Jewish tradition of that time… It is a Jewish book…because a Jewish spirit and no other lives in it; because Jewish faith and Jewish hope, Jewish suffering, and Jewish distress, Jewish knowledge and Jewish expectations and these alone, resound through it—a Jewish book in the midst of Jewish books (Leo Baeck cited by Sherwin 2001, 35).

I can give a personal testimony here. One day, when I was editing *L'Olivier*, I had an appointment with one of the greatest and well-known rabbis of France, Rabbi Josy Einsenberg. Einsenberg wrote many books and led the Jewish national French television program every Sunday. When I was in his office, he told me that the New Testament had become more and more important for Jews. For him the gospels are invaluable for the historic information about Jewish life in Judea and Galilee in the first century. He added, "Do you know that the Gospel of Luke is the oldest testimony we have in the world about a *Bar-Mitzvah*?" The *Bar-Mitzvah* is a very important ceremony in modern Judaism. There is no evidence that *Bar-Mitzvah* existed during the time of the Hebrew Bible; but in the gospel of Luke, there is the testimony of Jesus' *Bar-Mitzvah*: "And when He [Jesus] became twelve, they [Jesus' parents] went up there [Jerusalem] according to the custom of the Feast" (Luke 2:42). Young Jewish boys today similarly celebrate their *Bar-Mitzvah* when they are twelve. For Jewish rabbis, the Gospel shows that the Bar-Mitzvah existed two thousand years ago.

In Einsenberg's book about women in the Bible, there is a section on "Jesus and Women." He justifies this with this historical observation:

> If the rupture between Judaism and Christianity gave birth to two different and opposed religious systems, very often antagonistic, there is no such opposition between the two parts of the Book that is composed of the Old and the New Testaments. We must never forget that their stories took place in the same country and in the middle of the same people. In other words, the stories that are told in the New Testament belong to

Jewish history, took place among Jews, and except for Pontius Pilate concerned Jewish men and women. This is completely true of the Gospels, and it is also true for the greatest part of the New Testament scriptures (Eisenberg 1993, 379).

Eisenberg makes the point that both Testaments center upon the life and experience of Jews in Judea and Jerusalem, trying to understand their relationship with a God who is more than a tribal God. The continuity of this theme runs through the two "great parts of the Bible." It is here that one can locate the Jewish reader, who is an insider in both Testaments.

How to Recognize the Words of Yeshua

Yeshua's words remain universally attractive. Arnold Jacob Wolf, in Judaism: A Quarterly Journal of Jewish Life and Thought, contends that their authenticity is relative to their historical Jewish context.

> How, then, do we know which passages in the Gospels reflect the words of Jesus? There are several criteria for authenticity that most of the new scholarship employs: 1. The criterion of dissimilarity. If a passage reflects neither a contemporaneous Jewish view nor the practice of the early church, then it probably is authentic. 2. In apparent contradiction, the criterion of compatibility with first-century Judaism. 3. The criterion of multiple sources. If several evangelists (or Josephus) say the same thing, it is more likely to be the reflection of what Jesus did or said. 4. The criterion of compatibility with what Jesus did. Jesus' actions may (or may not) authenticate what he said. 5. The criterion of embarrassment. Nothing that would embarrass the writers is their own addition. If Jesus was said to be baptized by John, or said to have died an ignominious death, he probably did. 6. The criterion of translation. If the Greek seems to be a translation from an original Aramaic (or Hebrew) saying of Jesus, it is more likely to be accurate. All of these criteria are relative, though none is useless. The historical Jesus can be recovered with a high degree of plausibility, but scholars will disagree on his nature (Wolf 2001, 26-27).

Arnold Wolf, interestingly, not only discovers the Jew, Yeshua, but claims that this Jewishness unlocks the Gospels.

Of course, we care because Yeshua's message transcends Israel, without replacing Israel. This is often seen by modern Jewish thinkers as well:

> I never hesitate to say that I consider Jesus of Nazareth as a third authority, to place next to the interpretations of Hillel and of Shammai. It seems to me that a particular tendency in interpreting Jesus is coming to light. It is a question of the internalization of the Law where love becomes the decisive motivating factor (Ben Chorin 1983, 17).

Hillel, grandfather of Gamaliel (Bacher 1904, 397), the teacher of Paul, is considered today as the great teacher of the Second Temple period. Hillel was a man of love who always tried to find a loving interpretation of the law. Some have said that Hillel was more "human-centered" and Shammai more "God-centered" (Young 1995, 272). In the same vein one can read a very interesting paragraph written by David Flusser, professor at the Hebrew University of Jerusalem, who said:

> Those who listened to Jesus' preaching of love might well have been moved by it. Many in those days thought in a similar way. Nonetheless, in the clear purity of his love they must have detected something very special. Jesus did not accept all that was thought and taught in the Judaism of his time. Although not really a Pharisee himself, he was closest to the Pharisees of the school of Hillel who preached love, and he led the way further to unconditional love—even of one's enemies and of sinners (1997, 92).

Yeshua and the Torah

Although Christians lay special claim to Yeshua, from the second century onward there have been persistent misunderstandings of the Apostolic Writings. One example is of the saying of Yeshua in Matthew 5:17, "Do not think that I have come to abolish the Law or the Prophets; I have not come to abolish them but to fulfill them." The standard Christian interpretation became that Yeshua was "in himself, in his person, the fulfillment of the Torah," and he thus cancelled the *Torah*. But taking into account Yeshua's Jewish background throws a different light on this saying. Fulfillment is a Jewish expression used in the Jewish tradition and rabbinical literature. Bronstein defines this locution in this way: "The locution to 'fulfill' (*lékayyem*) the commandments is opposed to 'void' or 'annul' (*lévatel*) the commandments" (2001, 52). As Paul said in Romans 3: "Do we, then, nullify the Torah by this faith? Not at all! Rather, we uphold the Torah" (2001, 31). Thus, this saying does not countenance supercessionism, it contradicts it.

Yeshua's Authority

Yeshua is always accorded authority in the Gospels. That authority is legitimated through the law and the Torah. Since the time of Ezra and the establishment of the Pharisees, the Jewish leaders devised elaborate prohibitions to defend the mitzvoth (laws). For instance, the Torah says: "Do not cook a young goat in its mother's milk" (Deut. 14:21), but the Rabbis say, "You have heard, 'Do not cook a young goat in its mother's milk' but we tell you don't mix meat of a young goat and milk in the same meal." Yeshua used the same kind of interpretation and extrapolation of the Torah in the Sermon on the Mount. "You have heard that it was said, 'Do not commit adultery.' But I tell you that anyone who looks at a woman lustfully has already committed adultery with her in his heart" (Matt. 5:27–28). Do not commit adultery is from the Torah, the seventh commandment in Exodus 20. Yeshua's saying is not from the Torah, but operates as an extrapolation of the Torah. The great difference between Yeshua and the Rabbis concerns the chain of authority. A rabbi refers his teaching to other Rabbis.

The Jewish tradition is full of sentences as such: "Rabbi Johanan says in the name of Rabbi Jose" (Berachot 7a). Precedent is the logic that moves the Mishne. It is said that the rabbis of the Talmud considered that rabbi a thief who borrowed an idea from another rabbi without giving his source. Yeshua abruptly broke with this logic: "But I tell you that...." That is why the Jewish people were very surprised and said to one another: "He taught as one who had authority, and not as their teachers of the law" (Matt 7:29). Yeshua preached on his own authority. The Pharisees, therefore, were not happy because they "believe[d] that they had the authority to interpret Torah by virtue of the oral transmission of Torah from Sinai through the succession of prophets and sages from Sinai to their own time" (Bronstein 2001, 58). Since Yeshua was not one of them, how dare he interpret the Torah without being invested by the Pharisees and Scribes? Bronstein concludes: "Jesus apparently set himself up outside of this authority. He undertook to 'go it alone'" (2001, 59).

To conclude this discussion about Yeshua and his teaching, a Jewish Professor, Daniel Matt, currently working at the Shalom Hartman Institute in Jerusalem, says,

> Jews can accept Jesus, not the Jesus of the church or Jesus-Christ the Messiah, but the Jewish Jesus, a long-lost cousin who, for nearly two millennia, has been misunderstood and perhaps lonely. By appreciating Jesus as a Jewish teacher, a Jew affirms that the wisdom of Torah manifests itself in countless, unforeseen ways (2001, 80).

Implications of these Attractions

Yeshua's Jewishness and faithfulness to the Torah and to his people are known in Jewish scholarly circles, and have motivated some modern Jews to accept Yeshua while remaining within the Jewish community. That is why I agree with Bodil Skjott

> Given the movement's stated conviction that the early church was Jewish and that believing in Yeshua, the Messiah, does not turn one into an 'ex Jew,' the community puts identity and integration into mainstream Jewish and Israeli life at the top of their agenda (Skjott 1995, 41).

The Jewishness of the teaching of Yeshua is very important in the testimony of those Jews who have accepted Yeshua as the Messiah. It exists even in the testimony of those who have accepted Yeshua as an important teacher. The success of the Christian mission to the Jewish community depends on reconnecting with the early church, where

Messianic congregations worship in the Jewish style under the teachings of a Jewish Messiah.

Hindrances

Our survey of attractions showed that Yeshua's life and message holds a lot of potential to attract Jews. Unfortunately, this attraction is balanced against a multitude of hindrances or objections. I have classified them in several different categories in order to simplify my answers and the reading of this paper.

Hindrances about Yeshua

The first category of hindrance concerns the status of Yeshua himself. It disturbs most Jews to be told that Yeshua is a man and, according to the church, a God. In addition to this apparent departure from monotheism, many note that Yeshua has not fulfilled all the prophecy and what is required to the Messiah.

The Two Comings of the Messiah

The coming of the Messiah is a controversial topic and one of the most difficult points of conversation between Jews and Christians. For the former, the Messiah has not yet come. Pinchas Lapide gives a good insight as a Jew about the coming of the Messiah. He states, "I cannot imagine that even a single Jew who believes in God would have the least thing against that…Should the coming one be Jesus, he would be precisely as welcome to us as any other whom God would designate as the redeemer of the world. If he would only come!" (Braaten and Jenson 2003, 363).

Nancy Fuchs-Kreimer relates a story told by Rabbi Zaman Schachter-Shalomi that is an allegorical gloss on this old question:

> The Messiah finally arrives. Jews and Christians, after waiting for so many centuries, rush to meet him. The Jews cry out. "This is the first time you have come, is it not?" The Christians, raising their voices above the Jews, insist, "This must be your second coming that we have been waiting for!" The Messiah smiles wearily and waits for the noise to subside. Then, in a quiet and gentle voice, long suffering, He says, "My dear foolish children. I have come not once, not twice. I have been here hundreds of times. But you have all been so busy fighting with one another you have never even noticed" (2000, 205).

These two quotations are important since they imply that most of the Jews who refuse Yeshua today do so sincerely. To understand the Jewish denial of Yeshua's Messianic mission, we must go back to the difficult relationship between Jews and Christians.

> Why has Israel been so slow to recognize Christ as her Messiah? Has the Church herself been an obstacle to that recognition? It is understandable that Israel should have suffered under pagan Rome, when her temple perished in flame, when 700 noble young men, bearing the temple treasures, were made to grace the triumph of Titus, when in the time of Bar Cochba 600,000 of her people were slain by the sword. But when she wandered across the dreary centuries of the dark ages, hated by Christians, driven from land to land, her children forcibly baptized, or poisoned, or burned alive in home and synagogue, when she saw 18,000 of her sons burned alive under Torquemada in the Spanish Inquisition, when she saw the exile of 400,000 from Spain in 1492, the horrors in Poland from 1648 to 1651, when tens of thousands perished, can we wonder that she failed to understand the Christian message of redeeming love? Let us ponder deeply these words of Sholem Asch. "How can we believe that Jesus is the Messiah, when he has become the origin of everything evil and wicked that has come over Israel since his name appeared in the world?" is the painful cry heard in Jewish writings through the centuries. What wonder that the Jews have refused so stubbornly to drink from the well which has contained nothing but poison for them? The responsibility for this lies with those who have contaminated the spring of God with the poison of Satan and of death (Aston 1947, 233-234).

Universal Silence about the Ministry of Yeshua

A second historical argument refers to the Jewish silence on the ministry of Jesus: "The philosopher-historian Philo of Alexandria, who died around 40 CE, extends into this period, but his writings says nothing about Jesus. While some Dead Sea Scrolls may derive from these years, none mentions Jesus. Nor are books of the Apocrypha and Pseudepigrapha that arise from this period helpful" (Cook 2001, 9). It is important to place the ministry of Yeshua in its context. Yeshua came anonymously, he was not a famous rabbi, was not known by his contemporaries, and had a very short ministry, only three years and six month. This accords with Isaiah's prophesy:

> Who has believed our message and to whom has the arm of the LORD been revealed? He grew up before him like a tender shoot, and like a root out of dry ground. He had no beauty or majesty to attract us to him, nothing in his appearance that we should desire him (Isa 53:1-2).

Yeshua's Purported Anti-Jewish Sentiments

Some Christian and Jewish scholars have pointed to supposedly anti-Semitic moments in the Apostolic Writings, or the "anti-Jewish sentiments attributed by the gospel to Jesus" (Cook 2001, 13). But what seems like anti-Jewish sentiment, when looked at from the deep structure of the Gospel, is actually a link to the Prophecies in the Jewish Old Testament. Yeshua HaMashiach was a Jewish Mashiach who was born as a Jew, lived as a Jew, preached to the Jews, and died on the cross saying "forgive them, for they know not what they do." To say that Yeshua was anti-Jewish distorts his entire life. This image of Yeshua gained credibility more from subsequent Christian anti-Semitism than the Gospel itself. Gelberman understood very well this fact when he affirmed, "Jesus came from a very orthodox Jewish family" and about Yeshua's harsh words he added: "He was not really attacking the priesthood and the religious customs of those days, but was opposed to those Temple priests who were turning their holy mission into a business" (2001, 117).

Hindrances about the New Testament

The second category of hindrances is about the New Testament. Jews are very reluctant to see this text as inspired and part of the Bible.

New Testament's Chronology

Rabbi Cook voices a common objection to the accuracy of the Gospel record, based on what we know about the writing of the New Testament: "One to two generations elapsed between Jesus' ministry (30 CE) and the eventual completion of the four canonical Gospels (70-100 CE). Such an extensive hiatus raises doubts: how accurately did these writings preserve the realities of Jesus and his ministry" (Cook 2001, 4). From the Mission point of view, the time elapsed between Yeshua's ministry and the writing of the four gospels is a problem that is resolved by understanding the inspiration of the Holy Spirit. The Talmud gives us a precedent. The Jews affirm that the Halacha or interpretation of the Torah included in the Talmud was transmitted orally by Moses to the elders, who transmitted it orally for two thousand years before the Jewish Amoraim decided to put these traditions in writing. The faith we have in Yeshua's sayings and the faith we have in the sayings of Moses comes from our faith in the God Moses announced.

Who Are the Writers of the Apostolic Writings?

The Jewish people does not accept that the New Testament has been written by the apostles who were Jews, that is why they look at the New Testament as a very anti-Judaic book.

> The New Testament is a document of the Gentile Roman Catholic Church of the second, third, and fourth centuries, and that church has clearly revised the teachings of Jesus and the early stories about Jesus in order to give the Romans the benefit of all doubts and to make the Jews who later 'rejected' Jesus look bad (Wolf 2001, 28).

Wolf's statement expresses a common belief, but the scholarly consensus is that the gospels and the New Testament were written between the years 50 to 100 CE. The "Gentile Roman Catholic Church" did not produce them. If we date the establishment of the Roman Catholic Church, as we know her today, from the time when the bishop of Rome received full supremacy over all the other bishops, we get a date of around 538 CE, and we know the Gospels were already common reading matter by that time.

Use of the Hebrew Scriptures by the Apostolic Writings

From a Jewish perspective, the New Testament's use of the *Tanakh* seems puzzling. How can we say that Jesus fulfilled the Old Testament prophecies when at the very beginning of the gospel we see so many mistakes? How can we trust the New Testament when many quotations of the Hebrew Bible are wrong, coming from the Septuagint (LXX), which was inaccurate in many respects?

Abécassis gives the example of the reading of Isaiah in Luke by Jesus. He said that:

> We cannot trust the quoting of the Old Testament by the New Testament, because the authors misquote the original text. In Luke 4 Jesus preached in the synagogue of Nazareth; the text he reads is from Isaiah 61:1-3. But the biggest problem is that we cannot trust the text because Luke quotes the text with a lot of freedom; he is not faithful to the original Hebrew text [my translation] (1999, 114).

Giving accurate examples Abécassis adds:

> Luke has the right to interpret the text but not to change it. For example, he substitutes the sentence "to proclaim the year of the LORD'S favor" in verse 2 by "to proclaim (*kerixai*). He deletes the middle of verse 2, "And a day of vindication by our God" which is, in the original text, said towards Gentiles. In addition, he takes the sentence "to let the oppressed go free" from another text, especially from Isaiah 58:6 (Abécassis 1999, 114).

Michael Brown, in his book on Jewish reactions to the New Testament, also considers the objection that the New Testament misquotes and misinterprets the Old Testament (Buber 1991, 3-21). As Brown points out, when we contextualize the New Testament with other Rabbinic writings of the time, such as the Dead Sea scrolls, we find that the New Testament writers were following the era's pattern of 'modernizing" citations from the prophets and the Torah. And in this same line Sandmel says:

> The newer scholarship in the nineteenth century emphasized the human aspect of the authorship of the Gospels; indeed by admitting the possibility of error in the Gospels, many of them came to assume that all of the Gospel material was suspect, unless it was specifically confirmed by non-Gospel materials (2006, 52).

As Brown's contextual point makes clear, the authors of the New Testament used the text they had at their disposal. Two thousand years ago, there were no printed Bibles in every home. Scrolls existed in Jerusalem or in some synagogues, and in a random way among the Jewish diaspora in the Roman Empire. Most of these Jews no longer spoke Hebrew or Aramaic. Let us remember that since the 6th century BCE Jews learned Aramaic while they were in Babylon, and progressively, this language replaced Hebrew as their current spoken language. In the third and the second centuries BCE, those who did not live in the territories of the former Israel spoke only Greek. Thus, it was natural to use the Diaspora Holy Scriptures the majority of Jews used. This was the motive behind the translation of the Old Testament into Greek, effected by Alexandrian Jews. The *NIBC* affirms, "Probably there was no city, next to Jerusalem, in which the Jewish population was so numerous as in Alexandria" (Singer 1904). The resulting "Septuagint" or "LXX" is the "General designation for the Jewish-Greek Scriptures, which consist primarily of various translations of the books of the Hebrew Bible" (McLay 2000). We have a certain amount of information on this project: "According to the pseudepigraphic letter of Aristeas (130 BCE), the Pentateuch was translated into Greek 285 BCE by seventy-two translators (hence its title, Septuagint). This tradition was later expanded to include all the OT books translated into Greek" (Schäfer and Meerson 2008).

Thus, the disciples and first Christians, like the vast majority of Jews, used the Greek version of the Bible, and the Evangelists (Paul and other writers of the New Testament) naturally used the text at hand.

The Messianic Prophecies

Jews who have studied the so-called "Messianic Prophecies" extensively traditionally dispute the idea that these prophecies are about Jesus. I will not deal with every Messianic prophecy in this dissertation. I will, instead, show how generally to use the Messianic prophecies and apply them to Jesus. My examples will be Genesis 3:15 and Isaiah 53.

When the first parents sinned in Eden, a promise was given to them, "And I will put enmity between you and the woman, And between your seed and her seed; He shall bruise you on the head, and you shall bruise him on the heel" (Gen. 3:15). According to this text there will be a war between the serpent (Satan, the devil, see Rev. 12:9) and the woman, and one of the descendants of the woman will kill the serpent, "He *shall bruise* you on the head," but at the same time the serpent would succeed in killing him, "And you *shall bruise* him on the heel." The fact that the Bible uses exactly the same expression from the root *shuf,* "to bruise," as is translated in the NASB tells something interesting about the destiny of both of them.

> The two deaths were to be simultaneous, as is evident from the Genesis text. The heel would be struck by the venomous bite of the serpent simply because it is the foot of the woman's posterity that would crush the head of the serpent. Moreover, the play on words in using the

same verb *shuf* to characterize both attacks tends to substantiate this explanation. It is suggested, then, that these two actions, though one was a "bite" and the other was a "bruise" or "crushing," would come as the result of an act. In killing the serpent the posterity of the woman would run the risk of death. The act would be a sacrifice (Doukhan 1981, 47).

It is interesting to notice that two ancient Jewish translations, The Targum[1] of Onkelos and the Septuagint,[2] saw a specific human being in this text. Jacques Doukhan states, "The Aramaic Targums d'Onkelos and of Jerusalem, both of them refer to the Messiah in their commentaries on this verse" (Doukhan 1977, 37).

The text of Genesis is backed up by the famous text in Isaiah 53, where the suffering servant is presented as dying for the sins of his people (Isa. 53:4-6 JPS).

Most modern Jewish commentaries interpret this text to refer to the people of Israel, who will suffer for others. Leora Batnitzky among many other Jewish scholars affirms, "Biblical scholars have had much to say from a source-critical point of view about Isaiah 52:13-53:12 and about the identity of the intended servant. Textual evidence within Isaiah itself suggests that, indeed, Israel is the servant" (Batnitzky 2000, 206). Rabbi Sandmel summarizes the Jewish feeling about the death of the Messiah,

> The issue here is not whether the Jewish way is better, or the Christian way better, but only that these two ways are so different as to be to most Jews and Christians incomprehensible to each other. Most of us Jews never penetrate to the point of understanding what Christians mean by the atoning death of the Christ. Most of us do not accept it because it is so foreign to our basic intuition; those of us who achieve a tolerably correct understanding of it do not accept it because it is foreign to our convictions. (Sandmel 2006, 47)

However, the full chapter of Isaiah 53 clearly presents the suffering servant as an individual who suffers for his people, for God's people. Maimonides himself saw the Messiah in the text of Isaiah 53. In Maimonides' first letter written in 1171 to the Jews of Yemen contains a long dissertation about the Messiah, relative to a Yemeni Jew who

---

[1] Aramaic translation of the Pentateuch finished in the second century CE. (Hiebert 1987)

[2] Greek translation of the Old Testament finished in the 2nd century BCE.

claimed to be the Messiah.[3] In his description of the true Messiah, Moses Maimonides wrote,

> And Isaiah declares also that he will appear without knowing who his mother or his father or his family will be, because it is written: 'For he has grown, by His favor, like a tree crown, Like a tree trunk out of arid ground. He had no form or beauty, that we should look at him: No charm, that we should find him pleasing' (Isaiah 53:2) (1983, 101-102).

Maimonides, then, accepted that Isaiah 53 could be applied to the Messiah. Let's take up the discussion here with a lecture given by Jacques Doukhan in Jerusalem (Doukhan 2009). Doukhan first presents the structure of the second section of Isaiah, which goes from chapter 40 to 53. Analyzing Isaiah 52:13-53:12, Doukhan gives the chiastic structure of this section:

A. Exaltation of the Servant (52:13-15)

   B. Humiliation of the Servant (53:1-3)

      C. Atonement by the Servant (53:4-6)

   B^1. Humiliation of the Servant (53:7-9)

A^1. Exaltation of the Servant (53:10-12)

Jacques Doukhan explains that Isaiah does identify the servant image with the people of Israel in certain verses (Isaiah 41:8-10; 44:1-3, 21; 45:4; 48:21; 49:3). But the text shifts to an individual in Isaiah 49:5. Isaiah 53 continues the thematic shift to the individual: one who carries the sins of Israel.

In the Talmud there are also some applications of Isaiah 53 to the Messiah. In the tractate Sanhedrin, Rabbi Yohanan asks this question: "For the sake of the Messiah. What is his [the Messiah's] name?" Many answers are given, and suddenly it is written, "The Rabbis said: His name is 'the leper scholar,' as it is written, Surely he hath borne our

---

[3] The two most famous "post-Talmudic" Jewish rabbis are Rashi (1040-1105) and Maimonides (1135-1204).

grieves, and carried our sorrows: yet we did esteem him a leper, smitten of God, and afflicted" (Talmud 2007c, Sanhedrin 98b), which directly quotes Isaiah 53:4.

This idea is not alien in the prophetic texts. In Zechariah 12:12 it is written, "The land will mourn, each clan by itself, with their wives by themselves: the clan of the house of David and their wives, the clan of the house of Nathan and their wives." The rabbis asked questions about this text, "What is the cause of the mourning [mentioned in the last cited verse]? R. Dosa and other rabbis differ on this point. One explained that the cause is the slaying of Messiah the son of Joseph, and the other explained the cause is the slaying of the Evil Inclination" (Talmud 2007a, Succah 52a). The figure of the Messiah who is slain has clear Jewish roots.

Thus, the Christian of the suffering servant is not alien to the Jewish interpretative tradition. The large point is: the Messiah was envisioned by the prophets as a sacrifice.

Yeshua's Genealogy in Matthew

Yeshua's genealogy in the Apostolic Writings poses another problem for Jewish readers, who ask: How can Christians pretend that Jesus is the son of David when the Gospels affirm that Joseph was not his father because he was born from the Holy Spirit? In Isaiah, we read that Isaiah will be the Son of David, or more exactly, the son of Jesse (Isa. 11:1). This son of Jesse could be understood as king David, because Jesse was the father of David and the grandson of Ruth the Moabitess who married Boaz in Bethlehem and gave birth to Obed the grandfather of David. Isaiah wrote long after David's reign, and thus this son of Jesse is not David, but a descendent of David. In the same chapter of Isaiah we understand that this son of Jesse will be very special, but not as a king of Israel (Isa. 11:10). The nations will resort to him and he will be like a sign for the peoples, giving him an international, rather than a simply nationalistic, dimension. Later in Jeremiah we read that the Messiah would be David's branch (Jer. 23:5). This concept was very well known in Israel during the time of Yeshua; that is why the title "Son of David" was attributed to Jesus eight times in Matthew (Matt. 9:27; 12:23; 15:22; 20:30; 20:31; 21:9; 21:15; 22:42), three times in Mark, and three times in Luke. This underlines the importance of the genealogy given by Matthew. To understand the Gospel writer's intent, we have to keep in mind a few facts. This gospel is not the work of an historian; it is not a word-by-word record of what Jesus said or did. In fact, this gospel, like the others, was written later in the first century. I believe it was written before 70 CE, or the destruction of Jerusalem. Scholars are divided in two groups. The first group are those who accept that this gospel was written by Matthew-Levy son of Alpheus, a direct disciple of Jesus between 68 and 70 CE, just before the destruction of Jerusalem (2010, 133). The second group of scholars do not believe that the gospel of Matthew was written by the disciple of Jesus called Matthew-Levy, but by a Jew who believed in Jesus. These scholars say that this gospel was written between 95 CE to 115 CE (Osier 1984, 312). This means that the gospel Matthew was written at least forty years after the destruction of the Temple.[4] In any case, Matthew was written for Jews. That is why this gospel continually reverts to the Hebrew Bible with phrases like "it has been written by the prophet" (Matt. 2:5). It was important for Matthew to prove to the Jews that Jesus is the Messiah. Thus, as in the book of Genesis, Matthew starts his narration by the *toldot,* that is, the genealogy (cf. Gen. 5:1).

This genealogy is presented like a Jewish *Midrash Aggadah*, which is a method or genre of narration drawn from the biblical text (Newman and Sivan 1980, 132), indicating the mixture of history and sacred connotations that traverse Matthew's genealogy. For this reason, it repays to give it a close reading.

---

[4] The date of the ministry of Yeshua is very much in discussion. I follow many scholars who say that the ministry of Yeshua took place between 27 to 31 CE. I accept the traditional view that his ministry lasted 3 years and a half

1. The first verse gives the main characters of the genealogy: Jesus Christ, David, and Abraham. Matthew's intention is to show that Jesus is a "son of David" and a "son of Abraham." He is presented as completely part of the Jewish people, a descendant of Abraham, a "son of David," and the second Adam. It is not by chance that this genealogy traces the lineage from Abraham to Jesus via David (the genealogy of Luke goes upward from Jesus to God, via Adam.) Matthew, in fact, presents this genealogy in this way: Abraham-David-Mashiach (Christ in Greek). The first letter of each name gives an acronym A-D-M (Abécassis 1999, 52), and as known, vowels are not written in Hebrew. What we have, then, is ADaM, the first man created by God. In this way Matthew alludes to the belief that Yeshua is the second ADaM, an idea confirmed by Paul (1 Cor 15:45). With the advent of the Messiah, a new page is turned in the history of God's plan.

2. Jewish genealogies don't usually include women, but we have an exception in the first book of Chronicles, where the genealogy from Adam to the kings of Israel does so. Matthew names five women in his genealogy: Mary, Jesus' mother, and four others, all of them Gentiles or non-Jewish[5]: Tamar the Canaanite prostitute, Rahab a second Canaanite prostitute from Jericho, Ruth the Moabite, and the wife of Uriah the Hittite[6]. These unusual genealogical moves intimate the universal mission of the Messiah, who comes to save all peoples. In Yeshua is converged the sacred history of Israel and the universal history of the world.

3. The first section of the genealogy, from Abraham to David, is standard, but the second section, from David to the captivity of Babylon, seems to deviate in the sense that there were more than fourteen generations. The third part of the genealogy is a mystery.

---

[5] The fact that the Bible says that Uriah was a Hittite and not a Jew—although perhaps converted to the God of Israel—it is reasonable to assume his wife was a Hittite, too. According to 1 Chronicles 11, the army of king David was composed of many people from the surrounding nations, that is, Ammonites, Moabites, and Hittites, and others.

[6] Even if the Bible gives the name of the wife of Uriah, Bathsheba, the genealogy mentions her only as the wife of Uriah and not by her name

There are no records for some of the people who are mentioned there. The narration stops about 300 years before Jesus, and all the genealogical records of that time were lost with the destruction of Jerusalem.

It is safe to assume simply that Matthew passed over some generations. In the standard language of the time, the "son of…" can mean the real son or the grandson, or a spiritual affiliation. When Jews speak about the Messiah as being the son of Joseph, referring to the son of Jacob, that means he will live in the spirit of Joseph, his life would be parallel. He wouldn't necessarily be a descendent. Thus, Matthew's genealogy is constructed to show Yeshua's importance, his universal mission, and to enforce a numerological analogy. Matthew wanted to find fourteen generations between the three periods of the history of Israel. The first period, from Abraham to David, is the "patriarchal" period. The real history for Matthew starts with Abraham. Before him, the history of humanity was only a succession of failures, "five failures—Adam, Cain, Lamek, the flood, and the Tower of Babel" (Abécassis 1999, 48). The second period, from David to Babylon, is the royal period, and the third one, from Babylon to Jesus, is the sacerdotal period, when the Sanhedrin and the priests (sacerdotal) held power.

Why the number fourteen? This has to do with the *Gematria*, a Jewish numerological system. In the Jewish culture of Matthew's time, the number fourteen is the number of kingship, because it is the number of King David. David is written in Hebrew D-V-D. In addition, Hebrew has no specific signs for numbers. The numbers are the letters of the alphabet: *Aleph* = 1, *Bet* = 2, *Gimel* = 3, *Dalet* = 4, *He* = 5, *Vav* = 6, *Zain* = 7, *Chet* = 8, *Tet* = 9, *Yod* = 10, *Caf* = 20, *Lamed* = 30, and so on. Thus D-V-D in Hebrew is *Dalet* = 4 + *Vav* = 6 + *Dalet* = 4 = 14.

When Matthew, in accordance with the Hebrew texts of the time, says that there are "fourteen" generations between Abraham and David, he wants to put Yeshua as the main character of the Genealogy. He starts with Yeshua in 1:1 and finishes with him in

1:16. Yeshua is the king (1:14) of the patriarchal period, Yeshua is the king (1:14) of the royal period, and Yeshua is the king (1:14) of the sacerdotal period. The fact that there were fourteen or nineteen generations between David and Babylon was not important for Matthew, because it is a *Midrash*.

The Virgin Birth of Yeshua

Linked to the genealogy of Yeshua is his virgin birth. In Matthew we read: "Now all this took place that what was spoken by the Lord through the prophet might be fulfilled, saying, 'Behold, the virgin shall be with child, and shall bear a Son, and they shall call His name Immanuel,' which translated, means, 'God with us'" (Matt. 1:22-23). This quotation is from Isaiah 7:14, where it is written: "Therefore the Lord Himself will give you a sign: Behold, a virgin will be with child and bear a son, and she will call His name Immanuel." Since the start of the modern Jewish reading of the New Testament, this citation has been controversial. The word translated by "virgin" is עַלְמָה *almah*, which means "young woman," a married woman, because the word normally used for virgin is בְּתוּלָה *betulah*. The charge here is simple: Matthew must have changed the facts of Yeshua's birth to fit a misinterpretation of Isaiah. However, this objection seems rather crude. The Gospel writers were Jews, writing for Jews. If Matthew or other writers wanted to cheat their readers, the story of the virgin birth would be the last thing they would concoct. The LXX Greek translation the diaspora Jews read was, as we have pointed out, made at least 100 years before the birth of Jesus. The 70 or 72 rabbis who translated the Bible into Greek and translated the word עַלְמָה *Almah* by virgin (παρθένος *Partenos* in Greek) were evidently not working under Christian influence. It is important to check the use of the word עַלְמָה *Almah* in the Bible, of which there are seven occurrences (Gen. 24:43; Exod. 2:8; Isa. 7:14; Ps. 68:26; Prov. 30:19; Song 1:3 and Song 6:8). I will look at each of these occurrences using the Jewish translation of the Bible.

Genesis 24:43 states, "As I stand by the spring of water, let the young woman (עַלְמָה) who comes out to draw and to whom I say, 'Please, let me drink a little water from your jar.'" This verse is the narration of Abraham's servant who was sent to Laban by Abraham to find a wife for his son, Isaac, and found Rebecca near the spring of water, thus, his prayers were answered by God. The *Almah* (עַלְמָה) "young woman" according to the JPS translation is Rebecca. It is clear that Rebecca was not married yet, and still a virgin. The עַלְמָה *Almah* in this text is about a virgin girl and not a married woman.

The second text says, "And Pharaoh's daughter answered, 'Yes.' So the girl (עַלְמָה) went and called the child's mother" (Exod. 2:8). This verse is contained in the story of the rescue of Moses, who was in a basket of rushes, from the Nile. Moses' mother had put him there and asked Miriam, Moses' sister, to watch over him. When Pharaoh's daughter saw the basket, she took it, and then met Miriam who was asked to find a nurse for the child. In this text even the JPS translates Almah as "a girl." It is known that she was young and according to the Midrash Rabbah, Miriam was the first-born. She was five years older than Moses, and Aaron was three years older than Moses (Shemot, 1:13). It is clear that she was a virgin girl.

The third text adds, "First come singers, then musicians, amidst maidens playing tambourines" (Ps. 68:26). The Hebrew Bible uses the word in its plural form, עֲלָמוֹת *Alamot*. Most of the English versions as well as the JPS translate it "maidens," which in English signifies "girl or unmarried woman" (Crowther 1992, 543). Even in the Jewish translation, the equivalence of "maiden" and "virgin" is understood.

The fourth text unequivocally implies a virgin: "How an eagle makes its way over the sky; How a snake makes its way over a rock; How a ship makes its way through the high seas; How a man has his way with a maiden" (Prov. 30:19). It is impossible to imagine in the context of this verse that an unmarried woman, a maiden, could be other than virgin.

The fifth text, "Your ointments yield a sweet fragrance, Your name is like finest oil — Therefore do maidens love you" (Song 1:3). The word is in the plural, עֲלָמוֹת *alamot*, and exactly as in Ps. 68 and Prov. 30, and again maiden is used here, implying a virgin woman.

The sixth text also uses the plural form of the word עֲלָמוֹת *alamot*, "There are sixty queens, and eighty concubines, and damsels without number" (Song 6:8). The Jewish translation translates *alamot* by "damsels." For a non-native English speaker, it is not a word that is used very often. It derives from the French, which again is an unmarried and virgin lady. (Crowther 1992, 227)

The last verse is the text from Isaiah, "Assuredly, my Lord will give you a sign of His own accord! Look, the young woman is with child and about to give birth to a son. Let her name him Immanuel." This verse was kept as last to be sure that some conclusions can be drawn from all the other texts. If there was only this text, it could be difficult to interpret. According to the context of Isaiah 7:1, this young woman could be one of the wives or concubines of King Achaz who was afraid of the Aramaic armies who were coming from Damascus. He was encouraged by the prophet in receiving a sign; in fact, no one is really sure whom this girl is. She could have been a girl who was part of the harem of Achaz but who had not yet given birth to a baby. There would be nothing so remarkable about a young married woman giving birth. But the verse is about a remarkable sign. It is here that the other uses push us to the conclusion that virgin is strongly implied. In conclusion I would like to quote the NIDOTTE:

> That the Greek παρθένος (*partenos*) used by Matthew and by the LXX in Isa. 7:14 can mean virgin and that an עַלְמָה (*almah*) can be a virgin are sufficient for the fulfillment to be identified. The Old Testament need not anticipate in its prophecy every specific element that finds fulfillment in the New Testament (Walton 1997).

Close textual reading like this are firmly in the tradition of the rabbis who translated the Septuagint. Matthew following them cited Isaiah's verse to prefigure Christ's birth. Today most people prefer the Hebrew Masoretic text, but the LXX is our privileged source, since it existed at the time of Jesus and the first church.

The Trial of Yeshua

Another difficult text of the Apostolic Writings is about the trial of Yeshua, which has been used, in the Christian tradition, to associate all Jews with the death of Yeshua. Jewish scholars have pointed to apparent mistakes in the text. For instance, any accused person was given 40 days to produce his witnesses to defend himself. In the Talmudic tractate Sanhedrin it is written, "He is going to be stoned, because he practiced sorcery and enticed and led Israel astray. Let anyone who knows anything in his favor come and plead in his behalf" (Sanhedrin 43a). That is why Rabbi Cook says, "Nonetheless, while accepting these premises, the rabbis denied that Jesus' trial had been in any way speedy or unfair, for a herald had announced throughout Palestine for forty days." (2001, 14) I must disagree. Cook is right to speak of a normal trial, but the Gospels are showing a perversion of legal practices. Yeshua's arrest at night, his trial close to the feast of Passover, and his execution on the first day of the feast, are all violations of legal norms. The Gospel report of the last days of Yeshua show a man being incorrectly hustled to his death by a panicked leadership. We cannot smooth out what was crooked.

Unity of God

As we saw in the third chapter, there was a long tradition in the Jewish community that condemned Christianity as an idolatrous belief because of the doctrine of the Trinity. Rabbi Cook writes, "Ironically, therefore, the same Jesus who had designated the *Shema* ("Hear, O Israel: The Lord our God, the Lord is one" [Deut 6:4]) his preeminent directive could also be summarily accused of having denied Judaism's cardinal teaching" (Cook 2001, 13). The Medieval and Modern Orthodox objection is based on one of the main commandments God gave to Israel: "You shall have no other gods before me" (Exod. 20:3). Let me observe here that in the *Tanach*, the Messiah is identified with God often. He is called YaHWeH, "The LORD Our Righteousness" (Jer. 25:6). The child who is recognized as the Mashiach is also called "Wonderful Counselor, Mighty God, Everlasting Father, Prince of Peace" (Isa. 9:6). And God himself affirms that there is no savior but God, "You are my witnesses," declares the LORD, "and my servant whom I have chosen, so that you may know and believe me and understand that I am he. Before me no god was formed, nor will there be one after me. I, even I, am the LORD, and apart from me there is no savior" (Isa. 43:10–11). Yeshua, then, deserves to be called "Mighty God," as he was incarnated on earth in his humanity and ascended to be reintegrated as God. There is no contradiction between the divinity of the Father, the son and the Holy Ghost, and the unity of God.

The Trinity and Incarnation

> The Triune God is incompatible with Judaism, thus it is impossible for Jews to believe in the trinity. Indeed the Trinitarian formula merits the focus in our discussion that on the one hand it is inherently incomprehensible to Jews, and on the other hand it ascribes to Jesus a divinity, which Jews are unwilling to ascribe to any man (Sandmel 2006, 44).

As one can see with this citation from Sandmel, the divine nature of Jesus seems to present a parting of the ways with Judaism. Rabbi Aryeh Kaplan says: "For Jews the most difficult doctrines to accept are the Trinity, the Incarnation and the need of a Mediator" (Kaplan 1985, 24). It is a scandal for the Jews, not only Rabbis, but also for postmodern Jews:

> The particularity of classic Christianity has become a major "scandal," to use the New Testament word, not only to non-Christians but to many who call themselves Christians. To claim the identity (in the Trinity) of one particular man with the one God and to point to his crucifixion and resurrection as somehow literally saving humankind, affronts the modern soul with its universalistic sense of value. (Borowitz 2001, 191)

Borowitz is correct that the basis of Christianity "affronts the modern soul" by retaining the belief that the nature of God is a mystery. No one on the earth can truly say that he or she understands the nature of God, who God is, and what He is doing. The divinity of Yeshua was announced by he himself: "I and the Father are one" (John 10:30) or "Truly, truly, I say to you, before Abraham was born, I am" (John 8:58). However, the Trinity is not alien to the testimony of the Old Testament. I am speaking only about "evidence" because it is clear that the discussion will be open until the second coming of Yeshua. God remains as a mystery to man. He wants believers to have faith without always requiring proof for their faith. The Hebrew word for faith is *Emunah*, which is "trusting in" and "obedience" at the same time.

In the Old Testament, *Elohim*, and *Adonai*, the names for God, are plural. God speaks in plural form in one of the famous passages in Genesis: "Let Us make [נַעֲשֶׂה] man in Our image [בְּצַלְמֵנוּ], according to Our likeness [כִּדְמוּתֵנוּ]...." (Gen 1:26). Of course, different interpretations of this have been given: for instance, that it is a royal plural, used because God is King.

A second sign in the Old Testament is the description of the savior. Isaiah 43:11 reads, "I, even I, am the LORD; And there is no savior besides Me." To believe that a Savior could be merely mortal misunderstands the whole function and purpose of the savior. This chapter of Isaiah is very strong. In the previous verse it is written, "You are My witnesses," declares the LORD, "And My servant whom I have chosen, In order that you may know and believe Me, And understand that I am He. Before Me there was no God formed, And there will be none after Me (43:10). God has two witnesses: his people, "you are My witnesses"; and the Messiah, who is called "My Servant." God himself has chosen this servant. God has made this choice in order for people to understand and believe a very important truth, "I am He." These are very strong words in Hebrew הוּא כִּי־אֲנִי "because I am He." God the Father is HE (HIM), the servant. There are not two entities here, only one. The Servant is God and God is Him. If people believe that the Servant of God, who is the savior, is not God, then, by this verse, they do not really believe the Servant: they are not in agreement with biblical revelation. Isaiah 43 goes on: the Lord said, "It is I who have declared and saved and proclaimed" (43:12). Our God is called the "redeemer": "Thus says the LORD your Redeemer, the Holy One of Israel" (43:14). The Apostolic Writings teaches that Jesus is the one who forgives sins. In Isaiah 43 it states: "I, even I, am the one who wipes out your transgressions for My own sake; And I will not remember your sins" (43:25). Isaiah writes that God is the first and the last (41:4); and again the text says that he is the first and the last and there is no God beside him (Isa. 44:6). Other examples are in the "messianic prophecies." His name according to Isaiah will be "Emmanuel" (Isa. 7:14), which means "God is with us." That is strong evidence for the incarnation; Jesus is really, not symbolically, "God with us." At the annunciation Gabriel said spoke this to Mary (Matt. 1:21). Only God can save his people from their sins; Yeshua name encodes this promise, meaning "God saves." In Isaiah 9:5 we read: "For a child will be born to us, a son will be given to us; And the government will rest on His shoulders; And His name will be called Wonderful Counselor, Mighty God, Eternal Father, Prince of Peace." Among the names given, "wonders" could be translated also by "marvelous," "miracles," and is almost exclusively applied to God. Another name of this child is "Mighty God" *El-Gibbor* in Hebrew, or "Eternal Father" and "Prince of Peace," the one who gives peace. All these names and titles cannot be given to anyone other than to God himself. These are strong evidences that the Messiah belief, which is at the heart of Jewish prophecy, testifies that there will come a child who bears the name of God as the Messiah:

> Finally, it is Isaiah who teaches that this new age will be brought about by a charismatically endowed descendant of the Davidic line whose reign will be justice incarnate (9:5–6; 11:1–5). These passages were later to serve as proof texts for the post biblical notion of *the* Messiah (literally, "the anointed one"), a uniquely designated being with extraordinary powers whom God will send to introduce the new order (Gillman 2001, 253).

Zechariah's prophecy (12:10) is one of the strongest signs. It convinced me as a Jew about the divinity of Jesus *"they will look on Me"*, and also about the future blessing of God upon the Jewish people *"I will pour out on the house of David and on the inhabitants of Jerusalem, the Spirit of grace and of supplication"* who will recognize the one they have pierced *"they will look on Me whom they have pierced."*

In this text it is God who is speaking. He wants to "pour out" His spirit on the Jewish people. When they receive His spirit their hearts will be touched and "they will look on Me [GOD] whom they have pierced." The image of being pierced predicts the fate of Yeshua on the cross. When the Jewish people will look at he who is pierced, God said, they will look on Me. That means it is GOD who was pierced on the cross. I found in this verse one of the strongest identifications of the Messiah with God. In Talmudic tradition, this text is interpreted to be about the murder of the Messiah, son of Joseph (Talmud 2007a, Succoth 52a).

In regards to the Incarnation, this, too, is foretold in the Old Testament, where there are numerous "incarnations" or "apparitions" of God. In the book of Genesis, God can be seen coming to the earth appearing as an angel of God. There are texts that support these famous appearances: Genesis 18—three angels appear to Abraham, one of them is God; Genesis 32—Jacob struggled with the angel of God; Exodus 3—the appearance of God to Moses as the angel of God and called God; Exodus 23:20-24—a special angel who follows Israel in the wilderness. This angel has special power to forgive their sins (like the Savior) and bears in Him the name of God, which is very exceptional. That is why I have a tendency to believe that this angel is named in the book of Daniel as Michael, in Hebrew מִיכָאֵל, the one WHO = (Mi) LIKE = (KA) GOD = (EL). The role of Michael in Daniel is "to stand up" for God's people and to defend him. There is an identity of function between Michael and Jesus, who is the defender of God's people, the advocate of God's people who stands up for all. When we think about the incarnation of God in the Messiah, we need to remember that in the Hebrew Bible there is a description of two kinds of Messiah, the suffering servant, who is the Emmanuel (Isa. 7:14) who will be born in Bethlehem (Mic. 5:1) and who is a son of David, and a descendant of David (Jer. 23:5) who will suffer for the forgiveness of his people (Isa. 53:3-5), and then the second aspect of a divine Messiah:

> I kept looking in the night visions, and behold, with the clouds of heaven One like a Son of Man was coming, and He came up to the Ancient of Days And was presented before Him. "And to Him was given dominion, Glory and a kingdom, that all the peoples, nations, and men of every language might serve Him. His dominion is an everlasting dominion, which will not pass away; and His kingdom is one which will not be destroyed (Daniel 7:13, 14 NASB).

It is interesting to note that here the same words are used for the kingdom of God, "the God of heaven will set up a kingdom which will never be destroyed, and that kingdom will not be left for another people; it will crush and put an end to all these kingdoms, but it will itself endure forever" (Dan. 2:44 NASB). These verses tell us that the Messiah is in heaven, from whence he will come like a stone (Daniel 2), and He will receive from God the Father all glory and dominion over everything. How can these two different visions of the Messiah be combined if we don't want to fall into the trap of saying that there are two different Messiahs, the son of Joseph and the son of David? Following the logic of the prophetic writings, we understand that the Messiah is in heaven, is a divine character, and when it was time for him to come on the earth as the son of David, God performed the miracle that brought the heavenly Messiah to earth in the form of a man born of woman. This may defy science, but faith is at the limit of human wisdom. That the incarnation happens will never be comprehended by human wisdom. That is why in Jeremiah 23, this Messiah who is the descendant of David will bear the name of God: "And this is His name by which He will be called, 'The LORD our righteousness." In Hebrew there is no discussion possible "יְהוָה ׀ צִדְקֵנוּ." The name given is the Holy four unpronounceable letters of the name of God, called also the Tetragrammaton. Only God can bear this holy name. This interpretation is in agreement with the *Midrash* that says, "What is the name of King Messiah? R. Abba b. Kahana said: His name is 'the Lord'; as it is stated, and this is the name whereby he shall be called, The Lord is our righteousness" (Jer. 23, 6) (Talmud 2007b, Midrash Eicha Rabba 41:1).

On the theological side of this doctrine, there is also the issue of sin and its biblical solution. The very first narration about humans is about Adam and Eve's sin and the expulsion from Paradise. Inhering in this story is the notion of sacrifice. It is written "the LORD God made garments of skin for Adam and his wife, and clothed them" (Gen. 3:21 NASB). Commentators pondering the detail of the "garments of skin" note that such garments must be the products of killing animals. That was the first death in the history of humanity and this death was due to the sin of Adam and Eve. Through this first killing of animals Adam and Eve understood the seriousness of sinning against God. The first sacrifice entailed the first forgiveness: God did not strike down the first human couple. God forgives, that is the loving and merciful character of God, but God's justice has to be satisfied too. This is confirmed by the fact that in the second generation Abel can be seen making a sacrifice—an offering of animals unto God. Cain, who offers fruit and vegetables, cannot satisfy God's justice. After this passage, a whole history of sacrifice is unfolded in the Old Testament, from Noah to the patriarchs and up to Moses. In the books of Mosaic Law, the order of sacrifice is codified. The logic of sacrifice and forgiveness is established. God's people err—as they did worshipping the Golden Calf—and they sacrifice. God does not, however, "want" animal flesh.

The sacrifices are symbols of the sacrifice to come: that of the Messiah himself. "Surely he carried our griefs and bore our sorrows; yet we ourselves esteemed Him stricken, Smitten of God, and afflicted. But He was pierced through for our transgressions, He was crushed for our iniquities; the chastening for our well-being fell upon Him, and by His scourging we are healed" (Is 53:4-5 NASB). Sacrifice brings up the question of justice. How can human beings consider that someone dying for them could be an "act of justice?" If I am the sinner, and the sinner has to die, then why should someone else die instead of me? This dilemma can only be understood if people comprehend what God said in Isaiah 43, "You are My witnesses," declares the LORD, "And My servant whom I have chosen, In order that you may know and believe Me, And understand that I am He. Before Me there was no God formed, And there will be none after Me. "I, even I, am the LORD; And there is no savior besides Me" (10-11 NASB). There is no savior beside God, the savior is God himself. The salvation of humanity cannot be entrusted to any human person. It would have to be God, whose death would be sacrifice enough for all people. This is the central mystery of the Christian faith, which can only be understood by way of the law and the prophets. That is why when Jews are prophetically looking at the one they have pierced, they are looking at God himself (Zech. 12:10 NASB).

For Jews, this narrative is the most contestable Christian belief. In reading the *Tanach* and prophetic texts we find many signs that were signaled by the Gospel writers, who saw that the theme of sacrifice inheres in the story of the expulsion from Paradise. Sacrifice is at the heart of the dialectic of justice and mercy, and how these things are reconciled in God: "Righteousness and justice are the foundation of Thy throne; Loving kindness and truth go before Thee" (Ps. 89:14 NASB). When I think about this act of love and justice from God, my personal love for the triune God increases day by day.

God, then, is one with the Messiah, and the sign of that unity is the miracle of his incarnation on earth. He became like one of us in order to save us, as Paul observed:

> Have this attitude in yourselves, which was also in Christ Jesus, who, although He existed in the form of God, did not regard equality with God a thing to be grasped, but emptied Himself, taking the form of a bond-servant, and being made in the likeness of men. And being found in appearance as a man, He humbled Himself by becoming obedient to the point of death, even death on a cross. Therefore also God highly exalted Him, and bestowed on Him the name which is above every name, that at the name of Jesus every knee should bow, of those who are in heaven, and on earth, and under the earth, and that every tongue should confess that Jesus Christ is Lord, to the glory of God the Father (Phil. 2:5-11 NASB).

The Apostolic Writings

Jewish scholars have pointed to a number of problems with Yeshua's life story from the Messianic point of view:

- If Elijah, herald of the Messiah, had himself not yet appeared (Mark 9:11)—how then, could Yeshua be the Messiah?

- The prophets did not predict that the Messiah would be from Galilee—seemingly discounting Yeshua of Nazareth (in Galilee) (see John 7:52).

- Yeshua's descent from King David was disputed by some in the Gospels (John 7:40-42; cf. Mark 12:35-37).

- The question of Yeshua's adherence to the Law of Moses comes up in the Gospels as well.

- Yeshua was crucified, instead of leading the Jews to triumph over Rome.

- Jesus had been resurrected his followers insisted—but skeptics deny this claim outright (Cook 2001, 9-10).

Elijah the Prophet

Yeshua was asked about Elijah by his disciples. In response, he said, "To be sure, Elijah comes and will restore all things. But I tell you, Elijah has already come, and they did not recognize him, but have done to him everything they wished. In the same way the Son of Man is going to suffer at their hands." Then the disciples understood that he was talking to them about John the Baptist" (Matt 17:11–13). Thus, the promise given in Malachi 4:5-6 was fulfilled symbolically by John the Baptist.

Living in Nazareth

According to the *Tanach* the Messiah had to be born in Bethlehem (Micah 5:1-2), but no claim is made that he must live there. Yeshua was born in Bethlehem (Matt 2:1), and was the fruit of a lineage going back to David (see Yeshua's Genealogy in Matthew pages 90-94), but as a child he followed his parents who had moved to Galilee.

Yeshua and the Torah

The gospel does show that Yeshua was faithful to the *Torah*, and that he asked his followers also to be faithful to the *Torah*. His most famous command is included in his sermon preached on the Mount of Beatitudes: "Do not think that I have come to abolish the *Torah* or the Prophets; I have not come to abolish them but to fulfill them. I tell you the truth, until heaven and earth disappear, not the smallest letter, not the least stroke of a pen, will by any means disappear from the *Torah* until everything is accomplished" (Matt 5:17–18). The prophetic tradition made the Messiah a champion of the *Torah*, not its destroyer. However, what does that mean? The mission of the Messiah is to internalize the law of God in the hearts of God's people. The prophet Jeremiah says, "This is the covenant which I will make with the house of Israel after those days," declares the LORD, "I will put My law within them, and on their heart I will write it; and I will be their God, and they shall be My people" (Jer. 31:33). This was the message that Yeshua spread: the *Torah* is not an unloving document of rules, but a rule of the heart, given by God to Moses.

The Death of the Messiah

Rabbi Cook raises questions about the death of the Messiah that are often raised by practicing Jews, who assume that the promise of the Messiah is that he would be eternal and triumph over Israel's enemies. But this radically simplifies various beliefs about the Messiah held in the Jewish community 2,000 years ago, where the Messiah, in the apocalyptic books, is identified with the Suffering Servant announced in Isaiah. Opposed to this was another strain of thought that saw in the Messiah a national hero along the lines of David, and who would institute an eternal kingdom. In the centuries after the destruction of the Temple in Jerusalem, and the rise of Christianity, the Messiah of the prophets, the Suffering Servant, was replaced by the Zealot idea of a politically triumphant Messiah.

"For Jews", Rudin writes, "Jesus was not the Messiah because the expectations for such a personage were not fulfilled. Rome's power was not broken in ancient Israel; in fact, it became more savage and led to armed Jewish uprisings against the occupiers of the biblical homeland all unsuccessful" (Rudin 2011, 41). The belief in the militaristic Messiah led the leaders of the Jewish people to two catastrophes; the first, war against Rome, which ended with the destruction of Jerusalem and the Temple, and the second war against Rome in 132-135 led by Rabbi Akiba because he recognized in Bar-Cochba the Messiah. However, when spreading the word in the contemporary Jewish community, it is important to revisit the *Tanach* and its Messianic prophecies, reviving the different visions of the Messiah. The Jewish people know very well these two visions; one is called the Mashiach-ben-Yosef and the second Mashiach-ben-David. None of these

Messiahs have to make war against a civil power and overcome the human power. The Mashiach-ben-David is a glorious Mashiach (Dan 7:25), his role is not to make war but to establish an everlasting peace on earth (Isa 11:5-11), and the Mashiach-ben-Yosef is a suffering Mashiach who has to die for his people (Isa. 53). According to the prophet Daniel, he will be killed. Daniel 9 says, "The Anointed One [Mashiach] will be cut off" (27). Daniel tells why the Messiah has to die, "to finish transgression, to put an end to sin, to atone for wickedness, to bring in everlasting righteousness, to seal up vision and prophecy and to anoint the most holy" (9:24). The Zealot's version of a this-worldly, warrior Messiah is actually a historical novelty in Jewish history. It is not grounded in the Bible.

The Resurrection of the Messiah

The resurrection divides believers from unbelievers. Paul, who was not a direct witness of the resurrection, saw the resurrected Yeshua in a vision and was assured that more than 500 people had seen Yeshua after his resurrection. In a dialogue between Hans Kung, a Christian, and Pinchas Lapide, an Orthodox Jew, Kung asked Lapide to explain the resurrection. Lapide answered:

> With the utmost seriousness, as an Orthodox Jew, I must say that I cannot accept what you call resurrection, *kenosis*, and *apokatas-tis*, since this is not suggested by our Jewish experience of God. But neither can I deny it, for who am I as a devout Jew to define a priori God's saving action? To define means to assign limits, and this, from a Jewish standpoint, would be blasphemous (Küng and Lapide 1977, 481).

Historical Hindrances and Objection to Yeshua

How Yeshua has been accepted in history? Jews have not accepted it, and this is a great argument used by modern Jews to continue to reject him. It is essential at this point to consider these objections and to see if they are valid.

The Jewish Story of Yeshua, Toldot Yeshu

In the first centuries, as the Rabbis began to view the Christian Jews as sectarians and heretics, rumors were spread about Yeshua's character. In the Middle Ages, these scandalous stories were collected in a book entitled *Toldot Yeshu*. This book will be dealt with a little later in this literature review.

A Small Minority of Jews Accepted Jesus

We know that some significant minority of Jews in Judea and Galilee, in the time of Yeshua's ministry, and in the Diaspora, in the period described in Acts and Paul's letter, accepted Yeshua. The entire Jewish people cannot be spoken about here, because it is clear that the Jews who were living in Alexandria, Rome, and Mesopotamia (Babylon) did not hear his preaching during his three and a half years of ministry. The French historian Jules Isaac, who wrote two very important books, *Jésus et Israël* and *Genèse de l'Antisémitisme*, has shown that this minority was larger than is often thought today. Isaac was one of the prominent speakers at the Jewish-Christian Conference held in Seelisberg in 1947, and inspired the declaration known as "the ten points of Seelisberg"[7]. Rutishauser from the Gregorian University writes in an article,

> In order to prepare for this task, the commission had prepared ten teaching points. The form and content of these points were greatly influenced by the initiative of Jules Isaac who had presented to the Conference the manuscript of his book on the roots of anti-Semitism, *Jesus and Israel*. He had worked on this manuscript in the underground since 1943, after having been dismissed from Pairs by the Vichy Regime and after having lost his family members through the Gestapo deportations. The aim of his historical, exegetical work had been to clarify whether Jesus had rejected the Jewish people as a whole and whether the Jews had been collectively cursed for their rejection of Jesus as Messiah, as the churches were teaching. Isaac had summarized the results of his 500 pages of research into 18 theses, which presented Jesus in the context of the vibrant Jewish environment of his time. The influence of his work is evident in the ten

---

[7] http://www.jcrelations.net/An+Address+to+the+Churches.+Seelisberg+%28Switzerland%29+1947. .2370.0.html?L=3 (accessed September 10, 2012).

points which the Commission III document recommends (Rutishauser 2007, 43-44).

Jules Isaac pointed out that it is very important not to be misleading by prejudice, but to stay close to the reality according to the testimonies that are available. For almost 2,000 years, Christians and churches have accused the Jewish people of rejecting Jesus, of killing him. They even accused the Jews of deicide, or "killing God" (Isaac 1959, 349-385).

I believe that the New Testament, especially the four gospels and the Acts of Apostles, are historical books even though the purpose of Matthew, Mark, and John was not to make a historical report of what happened in Judea, Samaria, and Galilee 2,000 years ago. However, it is clear that Luke made some extensive research in order to find the truth about Jesus and to report exactly what happened (Luke 1:1-3).

If a person wanted to know what happened and what the attitude of the Jewish people towards Jesus was, the gospels are the essential entry point. Jesus preached mainly in Judea and Galilee among his people, who were very open to the proclamation of Jesus. From the very beginning we read that Jews were amazed by Jesus' words and deeds: "They were amazed at His teaching" (Mark 1:22). "And they were all amazed, so that they debated among themselves, saying, "What is this? A new teaching with authority! He commands even the unclean spirits, and they obey Him" (Mark 1:27, 28). "So that they were all amazed and were glorifying God, saying, 'We have never seen anything like this.' And He went out again by the seashore; and all the multitude were coming to Him, and He was teaching them" (Mark 2:12-13). Thousands followed him. There is the testimony of two multiplications of bread and fish: 5,000 attended the first one (Matt. 14:13-21) and 4,000 attended the second one (Matt. 15:29-39).

This positive behavior is the general attitude of the Jewish masses during Yeshua's entire ministry. A brief perusal of the synoptic gospels reveals that among 27 passages in Matthew where Yeshua is mentioned in connection with Jews, 23 are positive; among 33 texts in Mark, 29 are positive, and of 39 passages in the gospel of Luke, 35 are positive

Coming to the gospel of John, Jacob Neusner compares the gospel of Matthew with the gospel of John saying, "Matthew's picture of Jesus describes him as a Jew among Jews, an Israelite at home in Israel, unlike the portrait, for instance, given by John, who speaks of "the Jews with hatred" (Neusner 1993, 8). This gospel still has many positive texts about Jews regarding Jesus' ministry. Following are some verses of John's positive statements:

> John 2:23 "many people .. believed in his name."
> John 3:26 "well, he is baptizing, and everyone is going to him."
> John 6:2 "and a great crowd of people followed him"
> John 6:5 "Jesus looked up and saw a great crowd coming toward him"
> John 6:10-15 "about 5,000 of them, 'Surely this is the Prophet who is to come into the world' and make him king by force"
> John 6:24 "once the crowd realized, they got into the boats and went to Capernaum in search of Jesus"
> John 7:12 "among the crowds .. Some said, 'He is a good man.'"
> John 7:31 "still, many in the crowd put their faith in him."
> John 7:40-41 "on hearing his words, some of the people said, 'Surely this man is the Prophet.' Others said, 'He is the Christ.'"
> John 7:45-49 "no one ever spoke the way this man does"
> John 8:2 "where all the people gathered around him"
> John 8:30 "even as he spoke, many put their faith in him."
> John 10:40-42 "Here he stayed and many people came to him. They said, 'And in that place many believed in Jesus.'"
> John 11:45-48 "Therefore many of the Jews..put their faith in him..If we let him go on like this, everyone will believe in him"
> John 12:9-11 "Meanwhile a large crowd of Jews found out that Jesus was there and came for on account of him many of the Jews were going over to Jesus and putting their faith in him."
> John 12:12-19 "The next day the great crowd....They took palm branches and went out to meet him, shouting, 'Hosanna !' 'Blessed is he who comes in the name of the Lord!' 'Blessed is the King of Israel.'"
> John 12:42 "Yet at the same time many even among the leaders believed in Him" (Elofer 2000, 343-344).

According to John, Jewish leaders accepted Yeshua (12:42). A few days before the arrest and crucifixion of Jesus, the population of Jerusalem acclaimed him saying, "Hosanna to the Son of David; blessed is He who comes in the name of the Lord; Hosanna in the highest!" (Matt. 21:9). John presents Yeshua's enemies as the leaders, the priests, and the Sanhedrin, although not all of them. As we pointed out, Yeshua's arrest, trial and execution were illegal. This speaks to a leadership panicked by Yeshua's popularity. It is also fair to point out that the great majority of the Jewish people were not living in Judea/Galilee but in the Diaspora, which means Jesus did not preach to the majority of the Jewish people, therefore it was not the majority of the Jewish people who refused his message (Isaac 1959, 165-174).

Excommunication of Yeshua

Sherwin affirms one of the most difficult points for the Jewish people who are interested in the teaching of Yeshua by writing, "Most classical Jewish theological teachings express a negative view of Jesus" and "Jews, in effect, excommunicated Jesus from the Jewish faith and from the Jewish people" (2001, 31). As I have shown above, this negative view of Yeshua came out of the 'parting of the ways' of the second and third centuries, where the church and the synagogue each became more extreme. In fact, the church utilized Yeshua's teaching as a justification to persecute the Jewish people. Excommunication is not, of course, a term found in the Talmud. In this perspective it is interesting to remember that "while Jews have never accepted Paul's basic teachings about Jesus or the apostle's radical negative interpretation of the Torah, they have never 'rejected' Yeshua, as has often been charged. For example, the theologian and philosopher Martin Buber considered Jesus as a Jewish brother" (Rudin 2011, 40). The Jewish position about Yeshua has varied among Jews according to their degree of tolerance and religiosity. He was never, however, "excommunicated".

Many Modern Scholars and Rabbis have Not Accepted Jesus

The leaders of Jewish thought—the scholars and Rabbis—have expressed various sympathies with Yeshua, but in the end, only those within the Messianic Jewish community accept his claim to be the Messiah. We have listed some of the reasons for that rejection. However, the point here is that the rejection itself is a hindrance. It is important to remember that most of the rabbinic writings on the person and mission of Jesus until recently were produced in a polemic situation. From Constantine's time to the end of World War II, the Jews were persecuted by Christian churches, or with their complicity. The blood scandal was attached to all Jews as Christ-killers. In turn, Jews blamed Yeshua for the persecutions implemented in his name.

There is a historically true parable concerning this I'd like to cite. Around 1240 a converted Jew, Nicolas Donin, advocated, with the church, destroying Jewish books: the Talmud, Midrash, and others. A "disputation" was organized between Donin and four great rabbis of France. This happened on June 25, 1240. The text of one of the Jewish defendants is available. He says:

> Why do you reproach us so after gathering us here so you could contest our Law and set yourselves against our souls? It is because of this bandit [Nicolas Donin]...who has caused us our misfortune—but he is racking his brains in vain, because we would die for it [the Torah]; whoever touches it, touches what we cherish most deeply. And if your anger flares up against us, and we are dispersed across all the earth, won't our Torah then be found in Babel, among the Medians, in Greece, and throughout the several nations? You hold our bodies here in your hands, but not our souls, and you can eliminate the Torah only within your own realm (Dahan 1998, 33).

After giving this testimony, Gilbert Dahan says that following these debates the church drew up a list of 35 accusations against the rabbinical literature and many rabbinical books were burned on Friday, June 6, 1242, in a public place.

Today, for the first time in almost two thousand years, the situation is different. We live in a post-Holocaust era in which Christian churches, for the most part, acknowledge their guilt in past persecutions. Most of the Christian scholars are far from the Middle Ages polemic and are aware that the Bible cannot be read in the same way after the Holocaust (Turner 2009, 181-199). On the Jewish side, Jewish scholars can now approach the New Testament without feeling like the heirs of Nicolas Donin.

A pioneer of the new détente between Christianity and Judaism is Martin Buber. He was deeply engaged in Jewish-Christian relationships. He stated that the New Testament had been for him, for almost 50 years, his main topic of studies. On the same page of the same book he wrote:

> Since early youth I have sensed in Jesus my great brother. That Christendom considers him God and savior, I have always deemed a fact of supreme importance which I must seek to comprehend for his sake and for my own ... I am more certain than ever that he deserves a place of honor in the religious history of Israel, and that this place cannot be defined by any of the customary categories (Buber 1951, 33).

Buber added, "My personal and brotherly attitude with Jesus has been strengthened and purified and today I see it with a stronger and purer light than ever."

Shalom Ben Chorin, another Israeli scholar has written a book *Jesus my brother:* "Jesus is for me the eternal brother: he is not only the brother of men, he is also my Jewish brother" (Ben Chorin 1983, 12). Further on, Chorin says:

> I never hesitate to say that I consider Jesus of Nazareth as a third authority, to place next to the interpretations of Hillel and of Shammai. It seems to me that a particular tendency in interpreting Jesus is coming to light. It is a question of the internalization of the Law where love becomes the decisive motivating factor (1983, 17).

My literature review has turned up many such statements from 20th century Jewish scholars. Joseph Klausner, who we have mentioned for publishing the first book in Hebrew about Jesus, *Yeshu Hanotsri,* wrote in the introduction:

> If I can give Hebrew readers a truer idea of the historic Jesus, an idea which shall be alike far from that of Christian or Jewish dogma, which shall be objective and scientific in every possible way...then I shall know that I have filled a blank page (from the point of view of Hebrew

writers) in History of Israel which has so far been written upon almost solely by Christians (Klausner 1989, 11).

Klausner has also written some sentences which can shock many Christians, "Jesus was not a Christian; he was a Jew," and on the same page, "Jesus derived his entire knowledge and point of view from the Scriptures and from a few, at most, of the Palestinian *apocryphal* and *pseudepigraphical* writings and from the Palestinian *Haggada* and *Midrash* in the primitive form in which they were then current among Jews" (Klausner 1989, 363). To those who affirm that Jesus was very much influenced by the gentiles of Galilee, Klausner answers, "There were many Gentiles in Galilee, but Jesus was in no way influenced by them….Jesus spoke Aramaic and there is no hint that he knew Greek—none of his sayings shows any clear mark of Greek literary influence" (1989, 363).

The renowned professor at the Hebrew University of Jerusalem, David Flusser, in his book *Jesus*, writes about love:

> Those who listen to Jesus' preaching of love might well have been moved by it. Many in those days thought in a similar way. Nonetheless, in the clear purity of his love they must have detected something very special. Jesus did not accept all that was thought and taught in the Judaism of his time. Although not really a Pharisee himself, he was closest to the Pharisees of the school of Hillel who preached love and he led the way further to unconditional love—even of one's enemies and of sinners. As we shall see, this was no mere sentimental teaching (Flusser 1997, 92).

In the history of Jewish thought, one finds a spectrum of opinion. On the side of those who most oppose Yeshua, opinion ranges from those who have studied and strongly rejected Jesus and Christianity such as Maimonides, Rashi, and others who were living in a time of great controversy between Judaism and Christianity to those contemporary Orthodox Jews who see only harm in the deeds and teaching of Jesus. Among the latter is Rabbi Aryeh Kaplan who states in one of his books, Jesus was punished and humiliated as a troublemaker (Kaplan 1985). On the other side, there are those scholars who see the beautiful deeds and words of Jesus, even though they do not believe in him. In this group we can place some of the great professors, such as Flusser, Ben Shorim, Buber, Lapide.

Jesus Is Only One Among Many Other Messiahs

Along this line of thought Sandmel states, "Jesus was neither the first nor the last Messiah in the long history of Judaism by whom or for whom the claim was made that he was the long-awaited Jewish Messiah" (Sandmel 2006, 32).

Historically, it is correct that Yeshua was not the only one who was declared "Messiah." The New Testament openly testifies that Messiahs had proclaimed themselves before, and had proved false. Rabbi Gamaliel speaking to the Sanhedrin reminds people of Theudas and Judas of Galilee in Acts 5:36-37. After the time of the Gospels, the most famous Messiahs in Jewish history have been Bar Chochba, Sabbatai Zevi, and the Rabbi of Lubavitch.

Bar Chochba was recognized by Rabbi Akiba as the Messiah, and raised a Jewish army against Rome in 131 CE. This war was known as the second war of Jews against Rome (132-135 CE), the first being in 66-70 CE. It proved to be a total disaster for the Jews. Bar Chochba and Rabbi Akiba were killed, Jerusalem was razed, a new city was built on the same site, and a new name was given to the city, *Aelia Capitolina* (Hadas-Lebel 1990, 170). The name of the land of Israel became Palestine, after the name of the ancient Philistine people who inhabited the coast.

Sabbatai Zevi came much later, in the early modern period, and from 1648, when he started to claim that he was the Messiah, to 1666, Sabbatai amassed a considerable following in the Holy Land, the Ottoman Empire, and Europe. In that year, he came to Istanbul, apparently thinking that the Sultan would crown him as the king-Messiah. However, the Sultan, Mehmed IV, received him in a hostile manner. He gave him the choice to die or to convert to Islam. Sabbatai Zevi chose the latter (Merrill 1973, 161).

The third claimant for the role of Messiah appeared in the 20th century. Rabbi Menahem Mendel Schneerson, known as the Rabbi of Lubavitch, lived the last years of his life in New York and was respected by a large part of the Jewish people. He claimed to be a descendent of King David. He was one of the greatest rabbis of the 20th century, writing many books, advising hundreds of thousands of people, and purported to perform miracles. After escaping from Russia, he studied in Paris and then moved to Brooklyn, New York, with all his disciples. There he became popular all over the world for his miracles, his prophecies, and good advice to the ministers of the government of Israel. He died in 1994, but since that time his followers, who form a large cohort in the Orthodox Jewish community, proclaim that he is the King-Messiah and will come back to life very soon. Today thousands of Rabbi Schneerson's posters are everywhere in Israel, proclaiming that he is "our Lord, our Master, our king—Messiah always alive."

That a people who have a tradition about the advent of a Messiah will experience many claimants is a sociologically plausible fact. This doesn't invalidate the claim of Yeshua. More than a billion people have accepted Jesus as the Messiah; among them are hundreds of thousands of Jews. The latter are motivated not by any desire to separate themselves from the Jewish community, but on the contrary, to fulfill the message of Judaism, as they see it, by accepting Yeshua as the Messiah sent by God. It is not enough to say or to claim that this one or that one is the Messiah, as Yeshua himself pointed out. "By their fruits you shall know them." It is in this sense that the larger part of this literature review has been devoted to an analysis of the biblical and theological objections.

The Role of The Church in the Suffering of Israel

As can be seen from the many mentions of the persecutions of the Jews in this dissertation, an unavoidable objection to the Christian mission in the Jewish community is the historic guild of the Christian church in the mass persecution and murder of Jews. Rudin expresses this hindrance in the following way:

> As mentioned above, for centuries many Jews were wary of asking questions about Christianity, a religion that professed love, grace, and charity. But those qualities were generally lacking in the real world when Jews lived under Christian domination. Because of this negative existential reality, Jews often perceived the religion of Jesus as one of hatred, contempt and dread (Rudin 2011, 21).

I cannot help but agree with Rudin that the church bears a great responsibility in the suffering of the Jewish people. Even though many will disagree, it is important to know that for the Jewish people the Holocaust is an outcome of the "teaching of Contempt" of the church. I hope that the Christian mission to which this dissertation is dedicated is not taken to be blind to the crimes of the Holocaust, and that the mission is undertaken in the humble sense of the responsibility of Christians and the determination to never again renew this sinful and criminal attitude toward the Jews.

Existential Hindrances and Objection to Yeshua

These hindrances rank among the most serious missionaries will encounter, because they are about the existence of the Jewish people, their culture, their identity and values they defended during centuries to the point of martyrdom. If we don't understand their weight in the Jewish people there is no chance to touch their heart.

Jews Are Very Proud of Their Culture and Attached to It

"People are proud of their culture" (Hiebert 1985, 93). The first objection discussed in this chapter concerned the strong Jewish feeling of belonging to their culture. In my literature review, the question of the loss of identity and the loosening of the community bond seems to lurk below the theological questions. Partly, this is due to the message conveyed by generations of pastors and priests that Jews who accept Jesus as the Messiah and want to be baptized will, indeed, be separated from the Jewish people. This brings us to today's paradoxical situation: though the majority of the Jewish people today are not very observant, or are even absolutely secular, they remain proud of their community identity. Even in Israel, where the majority of Jews are not religious, to be a member of the people of Israel remains psychologically important.

As this data shows, what links Jews together is really their culture. They consider that their people and its culture have been built throughout a history of 4,000 years (since Abraham) and the result of this long history is the diversity of the Jewish people of today. Thus, coming to Christianity is a very difficult step for a Jew. While a converted secular gentile usually doesn't feel like he is 'betraying' secularity, a converted Jew may well fell like a traitor, leaving a four millennia culture for the side that has persecuted it. My own experience here is significant. When I began to think of accepting Jesus as my Messiah, it was difficult to consider leaving my culture, my people, my history and join a "new" people. When comparing any evangelical or protestant church with the Jewish people, there is no doubt that the Jewish people have a richer history and background. I retain this insight. I am very proud of what the "Jewish civilization" has produced during their history, even their biblical history. Therefore, I will not minimize the significant role of Israel in history. I remember that Paul wrote:

> For I could wish that I myself were cursed and cut off from Christ for the sake of my brothers, those of my own race, the people of Israel. Theirs is the adoption as sons; theirs the divine glory, the covenants, the receiving of the law, the temple worship and the promises (Romans 9:3-4.)

When most of the ancestors of the Western people were still living in very primitive conditions, the Jewish people flourished in a high civilization and had great kings such as David and Solomon, and an unsurpassed Wisdom literature.

Among Jewish writers, it is well known that the Jews gave the West not only the Bible, the prophets, the Messianic hope, the promises of God's kingdom, and the Messiah to them, but also an array of great thinkers, scientists, writers, artists, politicians, human rights activists, etc. Nobel Prizes provide an excellent index of Jewish success in the modern world: between 1905 and 2009, Jews received 53 Nobel prizes for medicine, 48 Nobel prizes for physics, 30 Nobel prizes for chemistry, 26 Nobel prizes for economics, 13 Nobel prices for literature, and 9 Nobel prizes for peace (Jinfo.org. 2011). 30% of the total of Nobel Prizes have been awarded to members of a population, which makes up only about 0.002% of the world's population—the Jews.[8] We remember here the blessings that God gave to Abraham, Isaac, and Jacob and their descendants (Gen 18:18; Gen 22:18; Gen 26:4). Even though these blessings have a spiritual dimension in Yeshua, they also have a literal dimension for the physical descendants of the Patriarchs. Christians must recognize that Israel is a blessing for the nations and the world.

I have also learned from the literature review that many Jews do not like Christian evangelism, which targets specifically Jews, because converted Jews are pressured to assimilate, and to lose their Jewish identity. When the gospel is proclaimed to the Jewish people and they are brought to Christ, it is vital to be very sensitive to their culture and their contributions to the world. Paul's words, quoted above, should be a model for the Christian mission. Paul loved his people, and knew from scripture that God loves them too (Rom 11:28).

Secondly, the literature review reinforces my view that the church needs to purge its latent anti-Semitism. How many times have I been told by a Christian that he or she

---

[8] Fifteen million Jews for a world population of seven billion.

was happy that, being baptized, I was no longer a Jew. As if Christians still want to eliminate Jews from the earth.

It is crucial to respect the culture of the people we want to reach with the gospel. One of the great missiologists of our time, Paul G. Hiebert, says:

> The gospel must be distinguished from all human cultures. It is divine revelation, not human speculation. Since it belongs to no one culture, it can be adequately expressed in all of them. The failure to differentiate between the gospel and human cultures has been one of the great weaknesses of modern Christian missions (1985, 53).

The gospel has often been too closely bound to Western culture, the European culture between the sixteenth to nineteenth centuries, and with the American culture of the nineteenth and 20th centuries. The great paradox in Jewish evangelism is that it is a gospel of return. Yeshua was born as a Jew and died as a Jew. The disciples were Jews, and the second part of the Bible called the New Testament was almost exclusively written by Jews; therefore, when working to bring Jews to Yeshua it is essential to respect their own culture. Christians as we have seen have often obscured the Jewish context of the Apostolic Writings, taking their cues not from Yeshua or Paul, but from Constantine. A contextualized mission to the Jews is, in a sense, also a catalyst to bring Christians back to the origins of Christianity. To quote a secular authority, UNESCO, on the autonomy and dignity of cultures:

> 1. Each culture has a dignity and value, which must be respected and preserved. 2. Every person has the right and the duty to develop its culture. 3. In their rich variety and diversity, and in the reciprocal influences they exert on one another, all cultures form part of the common heritage belonging to all mankind (Unesco 1967, 87).[9]

The modern missionary movement has rediscovered the interesting biblical principle of contextualization which is also called "incarnational ministry"(Hiebert 1985).

---

[9] Available in electronic form at http://portal.unesco.org/en/ev.php-urlid13147&urldo=do topic& urlsection=20.html (accessed July 8, 2012).

This is a biblical principle embodied by Yeshua himself. Paul talks of Yeshua's "emptying", and his divine human incarnation (Phil 2:6-8 NASB). Yeshua came down from heaven to save human kind as a human. We should go among those we wish to tell the good news in the form of their humanity, which is the basis of incarnational ministry. Paul wrote the following famous words in this regard:

> For though I am free from all men, I have made myself a slave to all, that I might win the more. And to the Jews I became as a Jew, that I might win Jews; to those who are under the Law, as under the Law, though not being myself under the Law, that I might win those who are under the Law; to those who are without law, as without law, though not being without the law of God but under the law of Christ, that I might win those who are without law (1 Cor. 9:19-21 NASB).

The literature review points out the numerous hindrances to "becoming a Jew to win the Jews". It also points out the attractions of Yeshua's message. I will propose a way of contextualizing in my last chapter on the "Mission to Jews," where the practical significance of my discoveries in the literature become clear.

Contextualization arose in the 1970s as a replacement for the "indigenous" paradigm (Hesselgrave and Rommen 2000). These authors spent long hours in research on this concept and have written, "There is not yet a commonly accepted definition of the word *contextualization*, but only a series of proposals, all of them vying for acceptance" (Hesselgrave and Rommen 2000, 35). Among the definitions given in their book, I like two of them. Bruce J. Nicholls writes that contextualization is "the translation of the unchanging content of the Gospel of the kingdom into verbal form meaningful to the peoples in their separate cultures and within their particular existential situations." And George W. Peters writes,

> Contextualization properly applied means to discover the legitimate implications of the gospel in a given situation. It goes deeper than application. Application I can make or need not make without doing injustice to the text. Implication is demanded by a proper exegesis of the text (quoted in Hesselgrave and Rommen 2000, 33-34).

In the context of the experience of my church, contextualization meant finding the form in which the content of the gospel is organically connected to the existences of the Jewish people in Israel.

First and foremost, this means always emphasizing that Messianic Jews are still Jews. Yeshua does not want Jews to cut themselves off from the Jewish community. On the contrary, he wants them to be "better Jews," like his disciples. Having discovered that Yeshua is he in whom the law and the prophets are fulfilled, they will believe in him as members of the remnant people of God.

Challenging Supersessionism

During the whole history of Christianity, the church, which followed Augustine in considering itself as *Verus Israel* (Simon 1996, 19), was not happy that Israel continued to exists. The church encouraged the persecution and killing of the children of Israel (crusades, inquisition, expulsions, bringing them down, lowering, degradations of their status,...) and a method of conversion that called for the convert to break entirely with the community. The church's position with regard to Israel followed the theology of "supersessionism." Irving Greenberg shows that this topic of supersessionism is related to hindrances because for Jews it is a way to discover if the message of the church is biblical or not,

> One of the criteria to discover if Jesus is a false Messiah or not depends on the Christian attitude towards Jews and Israel. Jesus is no false Messiah, that is, a would-be redeemer who teaches evil values. Rather, when Christianity, in his name, claims absolute authority and denigrates the right of Judaism or of Jews to exist, then it makes him into a false Messiah (Greenberg 2000, 156).

This hindrance is ties together theology and history. Christian anti-Semitism is a very live and sore topic in the Jewish community. One must answer, as a Christian, questions from Jews concerning whether Christians believe that Jews are still loved by

God, or whether Christians believe God rejected the Jewish people and put the church in Israel's place. If we do not answer these questions correctly, it will be very difficult to bring Jews to Jesus.

In doing mission work, we must be careful not to mix our understanding of the Bible with our personal feelings about what happens in the Middle East. When I speak about Israel, I do not speak only about the State of Israel which declared her independence in May 1948, but I am speaking about the Jewish people who are scattered all over the world, the legitimate descendants of Abraham, Isaac, and Jacob. The State of Israel is a Jewish state, but its actions and politics do not imply all the Jews all over the world. Jews are not necessarily required to support the politics of the State of Israel, but all Jews do support the existence of Israel. Evangelism need not deal with Israeli politics. On the other hand, it is impossible to avoid questions about the Christian role—either as passive bystanders or collaborators—in the mass murder of Jews in the Second World War. The six million murdered Jews stand as the darkest condemnation of a certain church encouraged anti-Semitism. In this trial, authentic Christians were those who defended the oppressed and persecuted, at the risk of martyrdom. David Bosch affirms rightly:

> Whenever the church's involvement in society becomes secondary and optional, whenever the church invites people to take refuge in the name of Jesus without challenging the dominion of evil, it becomes a countersign of the kingdom. It is then not involved in evangelism but in counter-evangelism (Bosch 1987, 102).

The evil fruit of supersessionism, the turning away from Paul's words, and Yeshua's, was the growth of an evil anti-Semitism leading to indifference or collaboration towards the murder of Jews. This was done under the excuse that somehow, Jewish babies, children, old people, young people, fathers, mothers, sisters and brothers were justly being machine gunned, gassed, tortured and beaten to death because "they" killed Jesus.

Supersessionism is thus supremely offensive to Jews. It is not an instrument to spread Yeshua's word, but 'counter-evangelism". In fact, Jews project onto Yeshua all that Christians say, preach, write, or do. They have this logical sequence in mind: "If the Church persecuted Israel, then Jesus must have taught the Church to persecute Israel." Jews, here, are applying Yeshua's words: through their fruits ye shall know them. "Thus who is anti-Semitic? The Christians? The Church? Jesus? Even though expressions like 'New Testament', 'New Covenant', 'New Israel', 'God of Love', 'Christian', and 'vengeful God' are biblical, they have some coloration of anti-Judaism or maybe they have been forged for this purpose" (Abécassis 1999, 27).

It is time for the church to be clear on her position on the Jewish people and Israel. I am in complete agreement with Kendal Soulen when he states:

> My treatment of the problem of supersessionism and Christian theology is shaped by four central convictions. First, supersessionism raises specifically theological problems about the truth and coherence of Christian faith and must therefore be addressed at the level of systematic theological reflection. Second, the effort to transcend supersessionism requires serious encounter with the theological claims of Jewish faith. Third, the systematic implications of supersessionism for Christian theology are best understood when attention is focused on the way in which Christians interpret the narrative unity of the Christian Bible. Fourth, when viewed in the context of the church's traditional understanding of the canon's narrative unity, supersessionism is seen to distort not only the church's posture toward the people Israel but other aspects of the church's faith and life as well (Soulen 1996, 3-4).

Challenging supersessionism, the church will open the door of God's love to the Jewish people and will help them to discover Jesus. This process will both renew Christians and deepen the Christian mission to the Jews. Christians should always remember, "Apart from a relationship to the people Israel, no relationship to the God of Israel is possible" (Soulen 1996, 8).

Summary

In the literature review we have discovered a constellation of attractions and hindrances that effect the success of the proclamation of the gospel to Jews. The attractions are about the life and message of Yeshua, his Jewishness and the writing of the New Testament. The hindrances are much more numerous, and explain why it is very difficult for Jews to accept Yeshua. These hindrances concern Yeshua himself, the New Testament, the historical development of the church and its vision of Yeshua, which definitely distances him from the Jewish Messiah. Finally, there are certain doctrines, which are difficult for Jews.

The following chapters will draw some implications from the founding and data of my research and my literature review.

CHAPTER 6

LEADERSHIP IMPLICATIONS FOR JEWISH MINISTRY

The purpose of this chapter is to analyze the organizational structure of the World Jewish Adventist Friendship Center of Seventh-day Adventists (WJAFC) in order to improve its operation and performance. In the first section I will describe some of my leadership principles, and then in the next section will use them to analyze the strengths and weaknesses of the WJAFC. Finally, I will propose some improvements.

Leadership Principles

A secular definition of "leader" is given by in an *US News and World Report* story as follows: "A leader is a person who motivates people to work collaboratively to accomplish great things" (2009, 15). This definition is broad enough to accommodate the sacred and the profane. The first factor in the definition is "motivation"—which is partly about incentives, and partly about commitment. The second factor is "collaboration". Organizations containing more than one person naturally rely on collaboration between members. The leader does not him or herself necessarily produce the organization's output directly. Rather, the leader motivates members to produce it in collaboration one with the other, committed to the terms and goals of the project at hand.

Finally, leadership has as its goal a value—"to accomplish great things." What is "great" is relative. The value could be economic, or it could be athletic—a winning team—or it could be sacred: gaining souls. Yeshua said, "what does it matter if a man gain the whole world if he lose his soul?" (Mark 8:36). This gives us a sense of the values in play here: the work of gaining souls is the work of gaining that which transcends the world. This, I think, qualifies as "great".

In working in a church setting, it is also crucial for the missional leader to cultivate awareness and understanding.

> The missional leader requires skills to cultivate three new kinds of awareness in a congregation. First is the awareness of what God is doing among the people of the congregation....Second is awareness of how a congregation can imagine itself as being the center of God's activities....Third is awareness of what God is already up to in the congregation context (Roxburgh and Romanuk 2006, 31-32).

Robert Banks and Bernice Ledbetter propose that Christian leaders understand that they are leading within an organization with a sacred purpose: "From a Christian point of view, it is only when the direction and the method are in line with God's purposes, character, and way's of operating that godly leadership takes place" (2004, 17). Plueddemann claims that Christian leaders "are fervent disciples of Jesus Christ, gifted by the Holy Spirit, with a passion to bring glory to God. They use their gift of leadership by taking initiative to focus, harmonize and enhance the gifts of others for the sake of developing people and cultivating the kingdom of God" (Plueddemann 2009, 15). These definitions put discipleship, the Trinity, the Holy Spirit and obedience at the center of leadership. Good leaders forego egotism, and glorify God the Father instead of their own talents. This humility sets secular and godly leaders apart. Leaders learn from their failure and errors. Speaking about humility Eddie Gibbs affirms, "Leaders are forced to learn through trial and error, and therefore should not presume to know everything in advance" (2005, 176).

Paul writes often about Christian leadership. For instance, he writes that leaders in the church "prepare God's people for works of service, so that the body of Christ may be built up until we all reach unity in the faith and in the knowledge of the Son of God and become mature, attaining to the whole measure of the fullness of Christ" (Eph 4:12-13).

Gibbs, speaking from a contemporary perspective, writes, "The primary task of the leader is to reconnect ecclesiology and missiology in order that the church be defined first and foremost by its God-given mission" (2005, 38).

Cross-Cultural Leadership

The mission to the Jews is by definition a cross-cultural enterprise, just as Paul's to the Gentiles was a cross-cultural enterprise. Sherwood Lingenfelter defines the such enterprises in this way: "Leading cross-culturally is inspiring people who come from two or more cultural traditions to participate with you in building a community of trust and then to follow you and be empowered by you to achieve a compelling vision of faith" (2008, 30). This describes the WJAFC situation. It is global, and it is composed of Jews from different countries and cultures. It is important to acknowledge that French or American or Russian Jews are different and we have to accept these differences. Lingenfelter says about cross-cultural ministry and leadership, "The vision essential for cross cultural leadership is based on an understanding of what the Scriptures teach of the kingdom of God and the vision that flows out of the power of the Holy Spirit to establish that kingdom now and in the age to come" (2008, 31). This is the apostolic gift and style, "...which recognizes that ministry in the surrounding community is increasingly cross-cultural and Christians needs appropriate insights and training for it." (Gibbs 2005, 49)

The World Jewish Adventist Friendship Center

The World Jewish Adventist Friendship Center was founded in 1998 as one of the Study Centers of the Seventh-day Adventist Global Mission or the Office of Adventist Mission. The first director was a pastor from Chile, but as he was a mono-lingual Spanish speaker, his communications with the General Conference were difficult and he resigned in December 1999. In February 2000, while I was in Israel, leading the work among

Jews, the General Conference contacted me and asked me to be the new part-time director of the WJAFC and to continue my work in Israel. Since my heart is in the Jewish ministry, I accepted their proposition and started to work as leader of the Jewish ministry in Israel and all over the world.

Jewish Ministry in the World

The work of the WJAFC started in 1998. In essence, before that date, the Jewish Adventist mission was non-existent. I took the direction of the WJAFC in 2000, when the extent of the organization consisted of: one congregation in Santiago (Chile), one in the Adventist University de la Plata (Argentina), two in Florida (St Petersburg, and Tampa), and one in Sao Paulo (Brazil). The progress since then is represented in these two Tables, which compare 1999 to 2012.

TABLE 10

JEWISH ADVENTIST CONGREGATIONS IN THE WORLD IN 1999

Countries	Congregations	Jews
USA	2	6,300,000
Chile	1	20,500
Brazil	1	100,000
Argentina	1	200,000

TABLE 11

JEWISH ADVENTIST CONGREGATIONS IN THE WORLD IN 2012

Countries	Congregations	Population
USA	25	6,500,000
Israel	24	6,000,000
France	1	600,000
Russia	1	250,000
Argentina	3	200,000
Germany	2	120,000
Brazil	6	100,000
Ukraine	3	80,000
The Netherlands	1	40,000
Chile	1	25,000
Uruguay	1	17,500

Where Should We Encourage New Jewish Ministries?

We have seen that Jewish ministries exist in eleven countries (Table 11). When we consider the plan of God for the Jewish people, this is a mere handful. I have made two more Tables: Table 13 shows our first priority new countries. Table 14 shows the second priority. Of course, being led by the spirit we cannot predict where ministries will arise with absolute certainty. We do know that the Jewish ministry succeeds only when we have leaders (pastors or members) who are trained properly to bring Yeshua to the Jewish community. We need to do that training, always conscious that second priority countries could give rise to those 'born of the spirit" whose ministries precede those first priority countries.

Consolidating the Existing Jewish Ministry

As Jewish ministries are already established in Table 11 countries, these are where we must strengthen and consolidate. My priority is to plant the seed in Table 13 and Table 14 countries.

TABLE 12

PROPOSED TOP PRIORITY FOR THE JEWISH MINISTRY: COUNTRIES WHERE THERE IS A JEWISH ADVENTIST CONGREGATION

Rank	Country	Jews	% in country	WJAFC
1	United States	6,500,000	2,10%	25
2	Israel	5,700,000	76,00%	24
3	France	600,000	0,95%	1
4	Russia	250,000	0,18%	1
5	Argentina	200,000	0,49%	3
6	Germany	120,000	0,15%	2
7	Brazil	100,000	0,05%	6
8	Ukraine	80,000	0,18%	3
9	Netherlands	40,000	0,24%	1
10	Chile	25,000	0,15%	1
11	Uruguay	17,500	0,53%	1

TABLE 13

SECOND SUGGESTED PRIORITY FOR THE JEWISH MINISTRY: COUNTRIES WITH MORE THAN 20,000 JEWS

Rank	Country	Jews	% in the country
1	Canada	400,000	1,18%
2	United Kingdom	300,000	0,48%
3	Australia	110,000	0,52%
4	South Africa	75,000	0,15%
5	Hungary	50,000	0,50%
6	Mexico	40,000	0,04%
7	Belgium	35,000	0,32%

TABLE 14

THIRD SUGGESTED PRIORITY FOR THE JEWISH MINISTRY: COUNTRIES WITH LESS THAN 20,000 JEWS

Rank	Country	Jews	% in the country
1	Italy	30,000	0,05%
2	Switzerland	20,000	0,26%
3	Belarus	20,000	0,20%
4	Spain	15,000	0,03%
5	Sweden	15,000	0,16%
6	Venezuela	12,000	0,04%
7	Austria	10,000	0,12%

How to Improve the WJAFC Work?

Looking around for models, I found John Kotter's "Eight-Stage Process of Creating Major Change" the most useful for envisioning mission expansion:

1. Establishing a sense of urgency,
2. Creating a guiding coalition,
3. Developing a vision and a strategy,
4. Communicating the change vision,
5. Empowering broad-based Action,
6. Generating Short-term wins,
7. Consolidating gains and producing more change,
8. Anchoring new approaches in the culture (1996, 21).

Establishing a Sense of Urgency

The Seventh-day Adventists based its mission from the beginning on the "Three Angels Message" of Revelation 14:6-12. They applied to the events of 1840-1844 the text saying: "Then I saw another angel flying in midair, and he had the eternal gospel to proclaim to those who live on the earth—to every nation, tribe, language and people. He said in a loud voice, "Fear God and give him glory, because the hour of his judgment has come." (Rev 14:6–7). This embodies the most urgent thing in the world: the Day of Judgment. This motivates the church to this day. Urgency is at the heart of the Mission.

Second Coming of Jesus

Jesus is coming very soon. This meaning of this notion, at the beginning of the nineteenth century, had been lost in most Christian churches. The Christianity of the day rejected a visible and personal second coming of Jesus.

The Seventh-day Adventist Church was born through a deep study of the books of Daniel and Revelation by one of her pioneers, William Miller. In the heart of the book of Daniel, the second coming is very well pictured (Daniel 7:13-14).

The second coming of Jesus will be visible and personal (John 14:1-3; Matthew 24:29-31; Acts 1:10-11; etc.)

The second coming of Jesus will be marked by the resurrection of the death (1 Thessalonians 4:13-18; 1 Corinthians 15:51-55; etc.)

The signs of the times given by Jesus and the apostles are fulfilled in our time (Matthew 24:3-28; 2 Timothy 3:1-7; etc.)

There Is Still a Mission to Fulfill

The mission of Seventh-day Adventists is addressed "to every nation, tribe, language and people"(Revelation 14:6). The people of the earth have to leave their false doctrines (Babylon) and to join God's people who remain faithful to God's revelation. In this sense, Seventh-day Adventists are in a position parallel to John the Baptist, preparing the way to welcome Yeshua back (Isaiah 40:3-5).

In this context, the mission of the church in regard to Israel is to bear witness in order to fulfill the prophecies about Israel's reconciliation with God (Isaiah 40:1-2: Hosea 3:3-4; Zechariah 12:10), being "grafted in" again in their own olive tree (Romans 11)

To Create a Coalition

We need to bring together a diverse group of people and empower them to create fruitful changes in the WJAFC. This group should be composed of top leaders at the General Conference, in each Division, and people who are currently involved in the Jewish ministry. The "key characteristics" of this team is *position power* (Kotter (1996, 57). As director of the WJAFC, I must try to motivate people to follow me in this coalition. For *expertise*, we turn to our leaders of Jewish Adventist congregation. They have led their ministry for many years, and know the Jewish community. Thirdly, to create *credibility* (see Kouzes and Posner 2007, 37) for the coalition, the members should be leaders at every level of the church, and have an excellent reputation in the church. This will facilitate cooperation from the top leaders of the General Conference. Fourthly, we require *leadership* to maintain our focus and sustain our action. Leadership is proven in performance, in the leading. With these elements, we can revive the WJAFC mission.

New Vision, Mission Statement and Strategy

No one company or organization can survive or fulfill its mission and purpose without a clear vision, mission statement and strategy. It is thus of the utmost important to define them succinctly and without coherently.

Qualities of a Good Vision and an Efficient Mission Statement

The qualities of the vision enumerated by Kotter are as follows:

- Vision is *imaginable* that means it conveys a picture of what the future will look like;
- It is *desirable* when it appeals to the long-term interest of the congregation and its members;
- It is feasible, when its goals are realistic and attainable;
- It is *focused*, when it is clear enough to be adopted by everyone and easy to be envisioned;

- It is *flexible* when it adapts to changing circumstances of countries and contexts; and
- It is *communicable* when it is easy to find language and symbols to convey it to the community's members (1996, 72).

WJAFC's Vision

To establish local contextualized churches, which will share the good new of Yeshua among Jews in a relevant way, helping them to accept Yeshua as the Messiah and working to be considered not as foreign organizations but instead as Jewish communities of faith, full of love and compassion for the greater community.

WJFAC's Mission Statement

The Worldwide Jewish-Adventist Friendship Center is an international organization dedicated to Jewish Ministries, fostering mutual respect, dialogue, understanding, education and research between Jews and Adventists. The closeness and similarities between Adventism and Judaism (lifestyle, Sabbath, Hope etc..) give them the unique opportunity to promote relations between Jewish and Adventist communities and dialogue at all levels, including bringing together Jewish and Adventist leaders and scholars.

WJAFC's Goals and Objectives

1. To provide a place of worship within the Seventh-day Adventist denomination for every Jew who is waiting for the second coming of Yeshua (Jesus) our Messiah, without denying their own culture and identity.
2. To work for reconciliation between Israel and the church Malachi 4:5-6.
3. To prepare the Jewish people for the second coming of the Messiah by comforting God's people and speaking tenderly to the heart of Jerusalem (Isaiah 40:1 5.)
4. To provide resources and training to help adventists better understand and welcome Jewish people, educating them about Anti-semitism, Dispensationalism and Supercessionism (through visits in churches, seminars, camp meetings, pastors meetings, colleges, universities).

The Strategy

A seven point strategy, innovating on earlier mission efforts, will help the Seventh-day Adventists to implement the Gospel vision among Jews. I would like to implement this strategy at the level of the World Jewish Adventist Friendship Center. I am organizing a World Advisory in 2013 and from the participants of this meeting I want to gather a coalition group who will think about the means of implementing the following strategy among the 45 Jewish Adventist congregation spread all over the world.

1. To communicate the new vision and strategies adopted by the coalition group, we need a specialized communication official who is familiar with the Jewish community and is experienced in change-producing communication.
2. A group of experienced leaders will be appointed to prepare and give contextualized trainings to the leaders of existing congregations and to pastors and members who would like to be involved in this ministry.
3. To make sure that each congregational leader follows a Hebrew course in order to be fluent in a sensitive Hebrew vocabulary necessary to ensure the context appropriateness of all preaching, teaching, evangelism, and Bible studies assignments organized in our Jewish Adventist congregation for a Jewish audience.
4. To ensure that our leaders continually improve their Hebrew speaking ability, they should be encouraged to study the Sabbath school in Hebrew; they may start with the Junior Hebrew Sabbath School lesson, which are easier to use because they include vowels. The Hebrew Sabbath School will be published every quarter on our website "Jewishadventist.org".
5. To communicate in a timely manner the gospel in its Jewish context to the Jewish people, we must begin publishing every week a newsletter and Bible commentary based on the weekly text reading, the *parasha*.
6. To survey our Jewish Adventist leaders and members in order to know who have health competencies (doctors, dentists, nurse, naturopath, nutritionist and so on) in order to create a training or correspondence course sensitive to the Jewish people and their Kosher lifestyle to respond to their special needs in health.
7. To invite each congregation to establish short-term goals such as a new church, small groups, Shabbat attendance, Bible Studies, and baptisms in order to help members and leaders connect the new vision and strategy to these important short run achievements.

Communicating the New Vision and Strategies

Changes in organization are never easy; employees, leaders and customers grow to depend on old routines and resist change. It is the same in a religious organization or a ministry. A good example is the way members of a congregation will arrive at church on Shabbat morning and go directly to sit down at the same seat week after week. That is why it is crucial for the success of this project to communicate properly about it to the higher organization and each level of the church (General Conference, Divisions, Unions, and Conferences and local congregation). I made communication the first point of the strategy listed above because it is the pre-requisite for successful change. Communication is a skill—that is why it is important to find someone with communication expertise. I agree with Kotter who analyses the "key elements" of an effective communication of the vision into content and form. In terms of linguistic form, we need *simplicity*, or lack of jargon, and metaphor *and example,* to give life and understanding to difficult concepts.

Illustrations are crucial to make difficult concepts easily understood. In terms of organizational form, we need *multiple forums* including big and small group meetings, newsletters, church bulletins, and other means to be sure that each one has heard and understood the project.

In terms of content, we need to encourage *repetition* of the message, which is the key element of teaching, as it normalizes at first strange term or approach. We need *leadership by example,* which satisfies the members' need for fairness. If we ask the church to adapt to more Hebrew-friendly congregations, the leadership must adapt too. *The explanation of seeming inconsistencies* is important to the credibility of the project: take questions! *Give-and-take,* or dialogue, is important. Leadership is not unilateral, and it is not communicated in monologs—it is interactive, and makes the community feels like they, too, own the vision, mission statement and suggested strategies.

Empowering Leaders and Church Members

As the community of the Messiah, it is very important for us to follow His teaching and His example. Yeshua was the master-teacher for his disciples. He first exemplified the ministry by teaching, preaching, healing, performing many miracles, taking care of poor, sick, and beggars. Then Yeshua empowered the disciples and sent them out (Matthew 10:16 and Luke 10:3). He empowered them with the Holy Spirit, "he breathed on them and said, 'Receive the Holy Spirit'" (John 20:22). And just before going up to heaven Jesus wanted to distribute this gift of the Holy Spirit saying: "But you will receive power when the Holy Spirit comes on you; and you will be my witnesses in Jerusalem, and in all Judea and Samaria, and to the ends of the earth" (Acts 1:8). Let us remember that "truly, a church requires a team building philosophy of leadership in order to bring together the range of insights, skills and experiences that are needed to translate vision into reality" (Gibbs 2005, 105).

Paul also empowered his companions and disciples. It is interesting to see the list of the functions Paul gives in Ephesians and how he describes their role,

> It was he who gave some to be apostles, some to be prophets, some to be evangelists, and some to be pastors and teachers, to prepare God's people for works of service, so that the body of Christ may be built up until we all reach unity in the faith and in the knowledge of the Son of God and become mature, attaining to the whole measure of the fullness of Christ (Eph 4:11-13).

This list shows us that every leader in the church has to consider his role as "to prepare God's people for works of service." We have to prepare and to empower our members to be God's people. "Only empowered people can reach their potential. When a leader can't or won't empower others, he creates barriers within the organization that people cannot overcome. If the barriers remain long enough, then the people give up, or they move to another organization where they can maximize their potential" (Maxwell 1998, 126).

How to bring about this empowerment? We must become better at training and discovering their spiritual gifts. Again, I agree with Kotter who said, "There are two common reasons why we fall into this trap. First, we often don't think through carefully enough what new behavior, skills, and attitudes will be needed when major changes are initiated...Second, we sometimes do recognize correctly what is needed but when we translate that into time and money, we are overwhelmed by the results" (1996, 108). The benefit we derive from training more than outweights its cost in completing the church's mission.

Generating Short-Term Gains

Bringing change in the WJAFC is a long-term challenge; I've outlined a program that puts a priority on garnering confidence and credibility from the members and leaders. I've also emphasized interactive communication: not only must the members bring about changes in the organization, but they must be sure that it is working and unafraid to However, one keeps up morale in an organization by making sure that members can see the short-term gains that a new program can generate, even if the program requires sacrifice. This builds confidence in the competence of the leadership and the rationality of the process. There will be resisters and skeptics at any level of the church, who have interiorized routines and don't want to see them go. They are not enemies. We reach out to them and to all by clarifying and redefining the process.

Examples of short-term gains include: new small groups, new people attending congregations and joining small groups, and new members joining congregation and accepting baptism. Kotter affirms that short-term wins produce pressure, and "pressure can be a useful way to keep up the urgency rate" (1996, 127).

Kotter attributes three defining qualities to short-term gains: (1) They are *visible:* they should be obvious for the members. (2) They are *unambiguous*: no argument is possible about the short-wins. (3) They are *related to the change process*: if the change in process opens a new page in the history of the WJAFC, all short-term gains must be in connection to it (1996, 122).

Consolidating Gains and Producing More Change

As I said it before, change is never easy, that is why we have to start small and go ahead incrementally, winning adherence from the leaders. As we advance, we achieve gains, consolidate them, and use them as starting points for more changes. The leaders in place will gain credibility from the organizational members, who will be excited about participating in visible progress in the organization. These incremental changes will change their own lives.

Anchoring New Approaches in the Culture

Even though the mission statement, vision and purpose of the WJAFC are culturally close to the Jewish culture, we exist as a part of a multi-cultural church. Each culture is driven by its own values. Jewish Adventist congregations have been planted in different culture (American, Russian, Argentinian, Brazilian and so on.), and as one would expect, mirror those cultures (which could be collectivist or individualistic, and so on.) We cannot touch certain cultural values of our congregations without raising opposition. As Kotter writes, "Most alterations in norms and shared values come at the end of the transformation process" (1996, 157). We want to contextualize our congregations for the Jews who live all over the world. It seems to me that Jewish Adventist congregations will accept the proposed changes, but it will be more difficult to get full agreement from the Conferences and unions, because they are suspicious about our ministry. Since the Seventh-day Adventist church has preached the gospel for almost 200 years without success among the Jews, it is crucial to communicate our success.

Coalition building reinforced through short-term gains can transform the mission to the Jewish community, casting off old methods and prejudices, and celebrating new successes in our ministry to Jews.

Summary

This chapter has focused on the place of the World Jewish Adventist Friendship Center within the Seventh-day Adventist Church. When the church established the Global Mission, it committed to reaching previously unreached communities. This commitment was renewed in 2005, when the Office of Adventist Mission replaced the Global Mission. The WJFAC was established in 1998. In 2000, I have been the director of this Jewish outreach center.

The Adventist Jewish ministry has achieved some impressive gains, establishing missions in 11 countries so far. Our vision is to reach the 30 countries where more than 10,000 Jews are living.

One impediment to the mission is that the leaders of the Conferences, Unions, Divisions lack faith in it, in spite of the record of success over the last few years.

A vision, mission statement and strategy (communicating the new vision, empowering leaders and church members, generating short-term gains, consolidating gains and producing more change and anchoring new approaches in the culture) have been established to revive the WJAFC mission as a living part of the church. This strategy can work if the leaders of the Jewish Adventist congregations commit to making it work. My next chapter will go further in the implication and implementation of all the founding of this research.

CHAPTER 7

THEOLOGICAL AND MINISTERIAL IMPLICATIONS OF MY FINDINGS

In this chapter my intent is to share the theological and ministerial implications of all my data, literature review, and research for the Jewish ministry. Since Paul's time, the church has been involved in Jewish ministry. Until the church in the second century turned against Israel, it was fairly successful in presenting Yeshua to the Jews. The book of Acts is full of the successes beginning with the baptism of 3,000 people on the day of the Pentecost. Yet as the church fell in love with power and became dominated by Gentiles, this history was forgotten. Worse, up until very recently, the church either passively or actively promoted anti-Semitism. Now, as the second coming of Yeshua is dramatically approaching, the church needs to return to the culture of the early church. With encouragement from the Word, I am sure that the church will have more and more success in Jewish evangelism because it is a promise from God (Zech. 12:10). God loves Israel, and he wants to share his Spirit with the Jews.

The work of God needs to be finished. Looking at the task, we know that by human means, it is impossible: but in God all things are possible. We can be the vessel for a special outpouring of God's spirit upon his children. In this outpouring the children of Israel will not be forgotten, they will receive the Spirit of supplication which will help them to be ready for the second coming. The prophet Hosea has spoken about this "return" of Israel (Hos. 3:4–5); this return is presented by Paul as "their acceptance" (Rom. 11:15); "they will be grafted in" (Rom. 11:23–24).

How to accomplish this? As this chapter proposes, we must discard the hateful image of the Jews as Christ killers—Yeshua died for the sins of humanity, and not because of the Jewish people—and we have to contextualize Yeshua for the Jews. It is important to present a Jewish Yeshua to the Jews in order to help them to accept him.

A Friendly Theology

Richard Groves tells this story:

> When "The Passion of the Christ" came out, the *Winston-Salem Journal* invited a local rabbi, a Catholic priest, a prominent African-American Baptist pastor, the pastor of the First Assembly of God, and me to be part of the first audience in our town to see the movie. In return for the free tickets, we agreed to return to the newspaper offices afterward and share our impressions, which would be included in a front-page story the following day.
> One of the issues the reporter wanted to explore was whether we thought the movie was anti-Semitic. He directed the question first to the rabbi, who thought for a moment and said, "I don't think the movie is any more anti-Semitic than the Gospels are" (Groves 2006, 223).

This story is not a surprise for me. Even though I know that the gospel is not anti-Semitic, the feeling of this rabbi is the general feeling among Jews. Perhaps this rabbi never read the Gospels. But the rabbi was applying what the church has done for two millennia to the Gospels, and imagining that the Gospels mirror this history. Many Jews claim that they do not need to read the Gospels to know if it is anti-Semitic just look at the teachings of the church, which arose from it. It is therefore very important to accept that Jewish evangelism must turn this reputation around, and be thoroughly friendly to Jewish culture in order to have a chance of succeeding.

To be friendly means to understand and to respect the Jewish feeling, their needs and their sensitivity. We have quoted Lapide, an orthodox Jew, above. In one chapter of his book on Jews, Israel and Jesus, he presents his research on "Jesus in Israeli Schoolbooks". It turns out that the presentation and the image of Jesus in the Israelis schoolbooks are very positive, and he concludes the chapter by a call to Christians to follow their example: "Might not the image of Jesus in the classrooms of Israel today serve as a model of tolerance, to shape the image of Judaism in Christian classroom in a more truly Christian fashion?" (1979, 69).

PICTURE 1: THE CHURCH	**PICTURE 2: ISRAEL**
The victorious and crowned Church is holding in her hands the chalice and the banner that overcomes the cross; she is looking with insurance at the Synagogue	The blind Synagogue defeated holds a broken spear, the blindfold express her refusal to recognize Jesus as the Messiah. She seems to drop the tables of the Law, the symbol of the "Old Testament".

FIGURE 6

REPRESENTATIONS OF THE CHURCH AND THE SYNAGOGUE IN THE CATHEDRAL OF STRASBOURG[1]

Christianity has not treated Jews in a 'Christian fashion'. I am not even speaking here about persecution. Rather, I am speaking of a still current rhetoric linking Jews to terms like "legalistic," "blind," "deicide," or "bloodshed". A very good illustration of this

---

[1] http://www.jmrw.com/France/Strasbourg/pages/20040708-084052_jpg.htm (accessed January 17, 2013).

Christian teaching is the representation of the Church and the Synagogue in the Cathedral of Strasbourg in France, built in the thirteen century (1230).

Christianity has not treated Jews in a 'Christian fashion'. I am not even speaking here about persecution. Rather, I am speaking of a still current rhetoric linking Jews to terms like "legalistic," "blind," "deicide," or "bloodshed". A very good illustration of this Christian teaching is the representation of the Church and the Synagogue in the Cathedral of Strasbourg in France, built in the thirteen century (1230).

Discard All Negative Views on Israel

A Jewish-friendly teaching and attitude should make a special effort to ban all kinds of anti-Semitism from its Christian teaching. It is important in this context to avoid preaching that God has rejected Israel. The Holocaust and Auschwitz has shamed most Christian churches into forsaking this language—but it is implied in the teaching of most of the churches. It is common to find citations such as,

> The church . . . as the people of the New Covenant has taken the place of Israel, and national Israel is nothing other than the empty shell from which the pearl has been removed and which has lost its function in the history of redemption (Ridderbos 1975, 354-355).

Another citation, "National Israel and its law have been permanently replaced by the church and the New Covenant" (Waltke 1988, 274).

How can people continue to think that way when they know the consequences and outcomes of this theology after the Holocaust? Van Buren admits:

> After Auschwitz, nothing in our hearts or our theology, if we would be disciples of our Lord Jesus, the Jew from Nazareth, can be as it was before, and any word or act that we Gentiles do that separates us from the least of his Jewish brothers and sisters stands under the judgment of Auschwitz, and therefore under the judgment of the cross. "As you do it to the least of these my brothers"—and please no spiritualizing, no mystifying typology, his real flesh-and-blood Jewish brothers—"you do it to me." My fellow Gentiles, how strange it is that you and I dare to pray

to the God of the Jews, to the one who willed to be known as the holy One of Israel. So when you pray, remember that the Jewish people prayed in Auschwitz as they went to the gas chambers, for had they not, what possibility of prayer would remain? The possibility, however, is there, and therefore we Gentiles can and may pray to the God of Israel. This means, moreover, that God's history with the beloved people, the beloved church, and the beloved world has not stopped, and that we are living at a turning point in God's history with us, which is also our history with God. That, too, is part of what we shall see when we finally find the proper place for Judaism and the Jewish people within Christian theology (Van Buren 1981, 127).

Unfortunately, some Adventist scholars have walked in this path of "replacement theology" or supersessionism. I completely agree, for example, with one of the most brilliant Adventist theologians of his generation and a professor at Andrews University Seminary, who said:

> Israel's election did not imply the rejection of the other peoples, but rather their inclusion. Israel was chosen, not just for its own salvation, but to lead the whole world to share in her saving knowledge and blessing. In short, Israel was chosen to represent the attractive character and saving will of Yahweh to the Gentiles (LaRondelle 1983, 92).

But I disagree with him when he says:

> If Israel would finally determine to be unfaithful to Yahweh, she would lose her privileges to receive God's blessings and be placed under the covenant curse, as stated so forthrightly in Leviticus 26 and Deuteronomy 28 (LaRondelle 1983, 93).

When and how can it be determined that Israel is faithful or unfaithful? The history of Israel in the *Tanach* is a story of successes and failures. Who has always been successful and not failed in the *Tanach*? Abraham? Isaac? Jacob? Moses? Even the ministry of Moses could be considered as a failed ministry. He freed Israel from Egypt, but during the forty years in the wilderness he did not succeed bringing Israel to obedience. God forbade him to enter Canaan. I agree with LaRondelle when he affirms, "Christ was the only perfectly obedient seed of Abraham, the only sinless Israelite who indeed deserved the endless blessings of God's covenant with Israel" (1983, 95). But this fulfillment of Israel's destiny in Jesus does not nullify the existence of the people of Israel. He came not only to fulfill the prophecies but also to gather "the lost sheep of Israel" (Matt. 10:6). He had a mission towards Israel; to gather Israel, not to replace Israel. That is why I am very surprised to read LaRondelle saying:

> Christ final decision regarding the Jewish nation came at the end of His ministry. When the Jewish leaders had determined to reject His claim of being Israel's Messiah. Christ words in Matthew 23 reveal that Israel's guilt before God had reached as completion (Matthew 23:32). His verdict was therefore: "I tell you that *the kingdom of God will be taken away from you and given to a people who will produce its fruit.*" (Matt 21:43 emphasis added). This solemn decision implies that Israel would no longer be the people of God and would be *replaced* by a people that would accept the Messiah, and His message of the kingdom of God (1983, 101).

By this logic, Israel has to disappear. Since Israel is no longer the people of God, since she has been replaced by another "people", the church should have no scruples in persecuting and killing Israel. "Replacement theology" bears in itself the gene of the genocide and the holocaust. That is why I am surprised to read such proud statements after the holocaust. It seems as if LaRondelle neglects to consider that "a long tradition of Christian anti-Judaism was a necessary condition for the Holocaust" (Earley 1981, 17). I am not arguing that Christianity was the unilateral cause of the Holocaust. Some scholars say that the anti-Semitism of Hitler was pagan and not Christian, and that may be true. But the perpetrators were, in the main, Protestant and Catholic Germans. The fact that a Protestant country as Germany could, in a relatively brief time, embark on the murder of the Jews was the result of a persistent "teaching of contempt" towards Jews in Christendom.

The church must be humble about it responsibility in the Holocaust, for centuries of anti-Semitic teaching, for her silence when the Jews were murdered, and for her collaboration with the Nazis in Germany, Austria, and other countries. Earley also affirms, "For the church, some Christian theologians have said, the Holocaust signifies a crisis of credibility due to the mass apostasy of the *Deutsche Christen* the almost total silence and inaction of the world's churches during the "Final Solution of the Jewish Question" (1981, 17). The evil seed of anti-Semitism at last bore fruit. We must never again allow that seed to be planted by, for instance, preaching and teaching replacement theology.

Positive Texts on Israel

The development of positive biblical texts on Israel could be the topic of a full dissertation. I, however, have limited my development to three key texts: (1) The fundamental text of Romans 9 to 11 affirming that God has not rejected Israel. (2) The concept of the eternal covenant that will never be removed in Isaiah. (3) The church will inherit together with Israel, not instead of or in the place of Israel, from Ephesians 3:6.

God Has Not Rejected Israel (Romans 9-11)

Most of the Christian churches have believed and said at one time in their history that God has rejected Israel and replaced her with the Church. Walter Kaiser wrote:

> The second Vatican Council described the Christian church as "the new Israel." A similar document titled "Report of the Joint Commission on Church Union of the Congregational, Methodist, and Presbyterian Church of Australia" also identified the church with "the true Israel." These citations are only a small representation of the reigning thought among many reformed and covenantal theologians today (2008, 41).

The pericope of Romans 9 to 11 has to be read in this context. Even though Paul regarded himself as the apostle of the Gentiles, he always preached in synagogues and was very concerned about the salvation of the Jewish people. This matter so troubled him that he started his pericope by expressing his sorrow (Rom. 9:2–3). Why was Paul so troubled? We understand that Paul wanted to see his people saved, but Paul puts the issue on a deeper level, asking in 11: "Did God reject His people?" (11:1). How can God reject His people? How can God change and deny His very being? God is, Paul writes, faithful to His people, but the members of His people are not unconditionally elected. Chapter 11 develops, then, he concept of the remnant (Rom 11:2-5).

This concept of the remnant is a universal concept from creation: Abel and Seth are chosen, not Cain; Sem is chosen, not Cham; Isaac is chosen, not Ishmael; Jacob is chosen not Esau; Elijah and 7,000 were chosen, not the other people of Israel; and this can continue throughout the history of Israel. Dan Johnson affirms that "the remnant is an essential motif for Paul's overriding theme of the salvation of all Israel" (Johnson 1984, 96).

Another theme in Romans 9 to 11 is the hardening of Israel's heart for a time. In the Bible, the hardening theme has a redemptive role, and it is what Paul said in chapter 9 about the hardening of the Pharaoh's heart (Rom. 9:17). In the same way the hardening of Israel's heart serves as salvation to the nations (Rom. 11:11–12). Yet, Israel's hard heart is only temporary and not permanent (Rom 11:12; 15).

> Paul makes it clear that the Jews' hardening is only temporary. Indeed, he rejects any notion of permanent hardness (v. 11) as strongly as he refuted earlier the idea that God had rejected his people (v. 1). In both instances he uses the same words: μη γένοιτο, "By no means!" Paul sees no need to argue the point further. He simply assumes that the temporary hardness will pass and the Jews will receive salvation. Their future full inclusion is as certain as is the fact of their present hardening. (Johnson 1984, 97).

The main idea of Rom 9 to 11 is that God has not rejected His people (Israel). The history of Israel is of remnants. Some branches are broken off—the Jews who refused grace and salvation offered in Yeshua—while others are grafted in—Gentiles who have accepted Yeshua (Rom. 11:17-18). Verse 11:23 marks the end of the hardening of Israel. If they do not stay in their unbelieving ways, they will be grafted in again. That is a grace from God. God has a plan for His people (Israel) until the end (Rom. 11:25–26). The Jews are the natural branches and it is written that "the natural branches be grafted into their own olive tree" and today it is the real problem, because natural branches have to "be grafted into their own olive tree." But that olive tree has been difficult to find; thus, it is very difficult for Jews to come back to Yeshua because they do not see it anywhere, this tree which is faithful to their original tree, faithful to the Torah and the Tanakh, a tree which does not betray their biblical culture and their biblical identity. God, Paul asserts, has a plan for Israel. He has never ceased to love His people and has never denied their election (Rom. 11:28-29). God is the same yesterday, today, and tomorrow; God is not changing, and that is the great encouragement one can receive from Him.

The Covenant with Israel is Forever

The only way to be sure about God's love is to see the permanence and persistent love of God for his people. I agree with Kaiser when he affirms

> How can the everlasting plan of God be trusted and believed in for the salvation of all people? If God—the same God, who based on His word and his own life (Gen 12:22; Heb 6:18)—once promised to Israel similar outcomes as those found in Romans 9-11, but has now rejected Israel and turned his back on them, what is left of the doctrine of the faithfulness and dependability of God? (Kaiser 2008, 42).

How can a person trust God if God is not faithful to his promise of love for Israel? We spoke of this in chapter 2. There, we did not analyze the topic of the covenant God contracted with Israel. Here, briefly, let it be noted that the promise regarding the covenant between God and Israel is an everlasting one (Gen. 17:7). This covenant is forever (everlasting) and is between God and the descendants of Abraham, which will be repeated to Isaac (Gen. 17:21) and to Jacob (Exod. 2:24). The sign of the covenant is circumcision (Gen. 17:10), and the land of Canaan is included in the covenant (Exod. 6:4). This covenant will be revealed to all the nations by the wonders God will make for his people (Exod. 34:10). Not only is this covenant forever, but it will never be removed and God's love for Israel as well (Isa. 54:10).

Israel Is Not Replaced by the Church

With Paul one can affirm that God has not rejected his people (Rom 11:1) and the church has not replaced Israel. Paul's epistles return to this question often, as though to underline his message. The purpose of God for the Gentiles is to be "heirs together with Israel" (Eph. 3:6), not instead of Israel. The church composed of Gentiles and Jews forms the mystical body of Christ, even though today they are two separate entities. However God's purpose is again to make one people with these two, Israel and the church. To quote Jacques Doukhan, they are "two voices for the same God" (Doukhan 2002). But the consequences are clearly expressed by Van Buren: "If the church stops thinking of the Jews as the rejected remnant of the people Israel, if it starts speaking of the continuing covenantal relationship between this people and God, then it will have to rethink its own identity" (1981, 118).

Biblical Foundation of a Positive Theology Towards Jews

After reviewing the positive and negative thoughts about Israel in the Bible and the prophecy, we may go on to establish the biblical foundations of a positive theology and behavior towards the Jews.

Relations of Comfort Between Israel and the Church (Isaiah 40:1-5)

God's plan for Israel involves the repentance of Israel and the community's acceptance of the Messiah. But God has given man a free will. From the very day of creation God created the human being with a "free will". Adam and Eve had to make a choice between God and evil. They had the choice to eat or not to eat the fruit of the tree in the Garden of Eden. In the same way, God will give to Israel the choice. Romans 11 speaks about the remnant, those who will accept Yeshua. I am not a partisan of simple or double predestination, and that is why I cannot believe that the "All Israel" is every Israelite, because God respects the free will of each individual. Each one will make his or her own choice to follow God and to accept Yeshua or not.

I deeply believe that the church is coming to repent her past vision of Israel and her relationship with the Jewish people, and is willing to change it. That is why I want to share a few texts that describe the new attitude of the church towards Jews. First, the text of Isaiah 40; this text is well known among Christians, especially verses 3 to 5, which are quoted in the Apostolic Writings describing the ministry of Yochanaan Hamatbil (John the Baptist).

According to this text there is a voice or a person who will come in the desert and will announce the coming of the Lord. He will prepare way for the coming of the Lord, acting as a precursor. The gospel applies this text to John the Baptist (Matt 3:1–3). According to Matthew, John the Baptist was this voice calling in the desert. But, in fact, not all the prophecy of Isaiah was realized in the time of Yeshua and John the Baptist, because in verse 5 of Isaiah 40 it says, "And the glory of the LORD will be revealed, and all mankind together will see it. For the mouth of the LORD has spoken" (v. 5). This part of the prophecy did not happen 2,000 years ago. It dovetails with the prophecy in the book of Revelation, which says "Look, he is coming with the clouds, and every eye will see him, even those who pierced him" (Rev 1:7). The text of Isaiah is a prediction with two applications: (1) at the coming of Yeshua, especially verses 3 and 4, and (2) the application that will realize verse 5 at the end of the present age.

The preparation for the second coming will be worldwide. It will be enacted by those who have already accepted Yeshua, which means the Church. The mission of God's people is in Isaiah 40:3-5 but also in verses 1 and 2. These verses are essential to understand the role of the church towards Israel. First, the church exists to "comfort" Israel. To "speak tenderly to Jerusalem", to speak to her heart. The church has failed to carry out the Lord's command during the last sixteen centuries. It is only by speaking to the heart and comforting Israel that the true nature of the Messiah will be revealed to the people of Israel.

The people of Israel have been accused by the church of "deicide" for the last 2,000 years. However, the majority of Jewish people were not in Jerusalem when Yeshua was condemned. And certainly no descendent, today can be charged with any sin in this regard. Verse 2 of Romans 11 says, "Proclaim to her that her hard service has been completed, that her sin has been paid for, that she has received from the LORD's hand double for all her sins." If there was a sin, Yeshua died as a sacrifice for it, as for all our sins. "Forgive them, for they know not what they do." The Lord wants to comfort her for all her suffering and the holocaust of the last centuries.

Relation of Reconciliation Between Israel and the Church (Mal 4:5-6; Rev 11)

The second, or complementary role of the Church is to reconcile, to bind together (Mal. 4:5-6). This text should be read in connection with the previous text of Isaiah 40 because it also relates to John the Baptist. When Yeshua announced to his disciples that he was the Messiah and had to go to Jerusalem to suffer and to be killed (Matt. 16:16-22), he was revealing his nature as the "Son of Man" (Dan. 7). The disciples were puzzled that the Messiah would have come because one prophecy would have not been fulfilled, the prophecy of the coming of Elijah. Yeshua then explained to the disciples that Elijah had already came (Matt. 17:11-12) and they understood that he was speaking about John the Baptist (Matt. 17:13). John the Baptist was, in fact, the Elijah who had to come. Two prophecies of the Hebrew Scriptures are about John the Baptist: Isaiah 40:3-4 and Malachi 4:5.

We have already seen that the church takes on the precursor role before the second coming of the Messiah. Her members are the ones who will announce the coming of the Messiah and will comfort Israel. But the complementary mission of the church according to Malachi is to "turn the hearts of the fathers to their children, and the hearts of the children to their fathers." Turning the heart in Hebrew means reconciliation. The second metaphor used in the text is the family relationship "fathers and children." Several interpretations of these expressions have been given; however, when this text is read in Hebrew there can be no doubt. The Hebrew text speaks about *abbot* and *banim*. *Abbot* refers to fathers, but not necessarily biological so much as spiritual fathers, just as *banim* refer to spiritual children. I understand that the mission given by this text to the Church is a mission of reconciliation between Israel and the church. This reconciliation is mutual. The text speaks of "turn[ing] the hearts of the fathers to their children," reconciliation of Israel with the Church, and "the hearts of the children to their fathers," reconciliation of the church with Israel. Thus, the mission of Elijah in the end time is to comfort Israel and to work on reconciliation between Israel and the church.

Christian Declaration for Dialogue and Reconciliation

To give comfort to Israel and to work for reconciliation between Israel and the church is the only way to help Israel to discover Yeshua. After World War II the church awoke to her responsibility for the pogroms and the holocaust. Partly, this was on account of the voice of Jules Isaac, a Jew who lost his family in the Holocaust and who wrote two very important books published after the war. The first significant Jewish-Christian dialogue conference was organized from July 30 to August 5, 1947, in the small Swiss town of Seelisberg and called "The Seelisberg Conference: The Foundation of the Jewish-Christian Dialogue." This conference was a milestone in the Church-Israel relationship. The attendees were 28 Jews (scholars and rabbis), 23 Protestants (scholars and pastors) and 9 Catholics (scholars and priests). At the conclusion of the conference they issued a 10-point statement known as the 10 Points of Seelisberg (see footnote 6).

This paved the way for the next significant step, the Council of Vatican II, when the cardinals and bishops voted on October 28, 1965 a statement called *Nostra Ætate*[2] to define the relation of the church to non-Christian religions. This declaration, addressed to the Jews, Muslims, Buddhists, and Hindus, had a revolutionary impact. In it, the Catholic church officially recognized, for the first time, that the Jews are not guilty for killing Yeshua. In the declaration read out by Pope Paul VI, it was affirmed that

> The Jewish authorities and those who followed their lead pressed for the death of Christ [cf. John 19:6]; still, what happened in His passion cannot be charged against all the Jews, without distinction, then alive, nor against the Jews of today. Although the Church is the new people of God, the Jews should not be presented as rejected or accursed by God, as if this followed from the Holy Scriptures. All should see to it, then, that in catechetical work or in the preaching of the word of God they do not teach anything that does not conform to the truth of the Gospel and the spirit of Christ (Rudin 2011, 100).

Many Protestant churches, among them the World Council of Churches, the Lutheran World Federation, the Lutheran Church of Bavaria[3] the Southern Baptist Convention, the United Church of Christ, the Presbyterian Church in USA, the United

---

[2] http://www.vatican.va/archive/hist_councils/ii_vatican_council/documents/vat-ii_decl_19651028_nostra-aetate_fr.html (accessed September 10, 2012).

[3] http://www.jcrelations.net/Christians_and_Jews__A_Declaration_of_the_Lutheran_Church_of_Bavaria.2377.0.html?&L=3 (accessed July 22, 2012.)

Methodist Church, and the Anglican Communion, followed these examples and started to publish their own declarations, admitting the evil of anti-Semitism, and urging reconciliation, comfort, or dialogue. Uniquely, only the United Church of Christ, in a 1987 statement, dared to wholly reject supersessionism: "Judaism has not been superseded by Christianity" and "God has not rejected the Jewish people." Other references are quoted by Rudin in his excellent book (2011, 96-103). Contemporary scholars recognize that Christianity and Rabbinic Judaism have the same origin.

> Historians of Christian origins are coming to the new conclusion that Catholic Christianity and Rabbinic Judaism are twins-exact contemporaries. Both were born in the first century, one following the Rabbi of Nazareth, and the other following Rabbi Johanan Ben Zakkai (who had also worked for a while in another Galilean town some twenty miles to the south of Nazareth and at about the same time as Jesus, but who had survived the siege and destruction of Jerusalem forty years later, and as an old man began the Academy in the town of Yavneh, from which developed Rabbinic Judaism). Both movements claimed the same father, and both were the children of one mother. That one mother was the postexilic implementation of Ezra's reform by the Pharisees. All those nasty things said about Pharisees in our Gospels reflect the later split between the young church and the young Rabbinic Judaism. They mask the evidence in their own sources that the Jesus-movement was, in its origins, an offshoot of Pharisaic Judaism (Van Buren 1981, 118).

The Methodist statement affirms "the persecution by Christians of Jews throughout centuries calls for clear repentance" and also "the understanding of the relationship of land and peoplehood, suggest that a new dimension in dialogue with Jews is needed." The United Methodists published in 1996 a statement where they affirmed, "the covenant God established with the Jewish people through Abraham, Moses, and others continues because it is an eternal covenant. Paul proclaims that the gift and call of God to the Jews is irrevocable" (Rom. 11:29).

Pope John Paul II declared "anti-Semitism...has been repeatedly condemned by the Catholic teaching as incompatible with Christ's teaching.. Where there was ignorance and…prejudice…there is now growing mutual knowledge, appreciation and respect" (Cited by Rudin 2011, 103).

The Seventh-day Adventists too have published some statements. First, the German and Austrian Seventh-day Adventist church asked forgiveness for what they had done and what was not done to save more people. In their statement they said:

> That by our failure we became guilty towards the Jewish people, towards all persons persecuted and all suffering of war and also towards Adventists in other countries. For this we humbly ask God and the survivors concerned to forgive us.[4]

Second, the World Jewish Adventist Friendship Center issued a statement at their World Advisory in Jerusalem February 2006, and reapproved it at the World Advisory in Buenos Aires, Argentina, in August 2008. Point 2 of this statement affirms:

> We as Seventh-day Adventists have much for which to repent in how we have related to Jews. Anti-Judaism and even anti-Semitism, rather than true brotherhood and acknowledgment of commonly held spiritual truths, have too often characterized our relationships. For this we ask forgiveness from those Jews affected by our actions (Elofer 2009, 202).

Jewish Answers to Christian Statements

It is important also to consider Jewish answers to the above statements. They will not be exhaustive but will give an overview of the main reactions.

In 2000, a council of 220 Jews (scholars and Rabbis) marked the thirty-fifth anniversary of Vatican II and the adoption of *Nostra Ætate* with a text entitled the *Dabru Emet*[5] (speaking truth) with eight points addressed to Christian Churches:

1. Jews and Christians worship the same God.

---

[4] http://www.adventisten.de/ueber-uns/dokumente-und-stellungnahmen/ (accessed January 17, 2013).

[5] http://www.jcrelations.net/Dabru_Emet_-_A_Jewish_Statement_on_Christians_and_Christianity.2395.0.html (accessed September 10, 2012).

2. Jews and Christians seek authority from the same book—the Bible (what Jews call "Tanakh" and Christians call the "Old Testament").
3. Christians can respect the claim of the Jewish people upon the land of Israel.
4. Jews and Christians accept the moral principles of Torah.
5. Nazism was not a Christian phenomenon.
6. The humanly irreconcilable difference between Jews and Christians will not be settled until God redeems the entire world as promised in Scripture.
7. A new relationship between Jews and Christians will not weaken Jewish practice.
8. Jews and Christians must work together for justice and peace.

The second landmark document illuminating the moment of détente came out in July 2009, issued by the International Council of Christians and Jews (ICCJ) to commemorate the Seelisberg Conference.

The 10 points of Seelisberg were addressed to the Christian communities as an answer to the Holocaust. The ICCJ Berlin document[6] has 12 points: four points addressed to the Christian communities, four to the Jewish communities, and four to both of them.

All these statements issued by Jews and Christians could be considered a "sign of the time", encouraging a positive theology and positive behavior towards Jews.

A Contextualized Ministry

The only way to reach the Jewish people is through a contextualized ministry. This ministry is not new. In fact, it goes back to the beginning, when Yeshua came as a simple Jewish man (Phil. 2:2-5) in a totally Jewish context. This context conditioned the writing of the Gospels. David Bosch wrote about the gospel of Matthew,

> His method was to rewrite the story of Jesus, with consistent utilization of written and oral traditions. While remaining true to what had been delivered to him, he nevertheless composed his gospel in such a way as to make it resonate for his own community (Elofer 2009, 202).

---

[6] Source: http://www.iccj.org/?id=3595, (accessed July 23, 2012).

Some Christians fear the contextualized mission leads to syncretism, combining Yeshua's massage and non-biblical beliefs and practices. It is a legitimate to fear pagan contamination of the biblical religion. That is why Paul Hiebert wrote about "critical contextualization."

> What checks do we have to assure us that critical contextualization will not lead us astray? We must recognize that contextualization itself is an ongoing process. On the one hand, the world in which people live is constantly changing, raising new questions that need to be addressed. On the other, our understandings of the gospel and its application to our lives is partial. Through continued study and spiritual growth, we should, however, come to a greater understanding of the truth (Bosch 1984, 19).

In another article Hiebert gives a figure to illustrate the different types of contextualization and the four steps necessary for a sound analysis.

FIGURE 7

TYPE OF CONTEXTUALIZATION
(Hiebert 1987, 111)

The contextual mission begins by gathering as much information as possible about the culture of the people one hopes to reach. Culture means their beliefs, their rituals, their stories, their songs, their customs, and their expressions of art or music—in short, their worldview. The pastor or missionary has to dig deep into the Bible to study what the Bible says about these "events" and what a biblical worldview is in order to evaluate the culture (beliefs, rituals, stories, songs, customs, and so on.) of the culture one is going to teach in. Only then can the community create a new contextualized practice in harmony with the Bible.

TABLE 15

APPROPRIATE VOCABULARY
(Elofer 2009, 145, 146)

Christian Words	To Be Replaced By
Old Testament	*Tanach* or Hebrew Scriptures
Baptism	Immersion, in Hebrew *Tevila*
Christian	Believer
Christ, Savior	Messiah or Yeshua or Jesus
Conversion	*Teshuva*
Cross, Christmas	To be avoided
Church	Temple–in Hebrew *Kehila*–Assembly of Believers
Home Group	Group of friends
A Converted Jew	Jew who did *Teshuva* full expression in Hebrew: *Baal Teshuva*
New Testament	Apostolic Writings in Hebrew *Brit Hachadasha*
Palestine	Israel
Pastor/Priest	A biblical teacher
Evangelism	Biblical meetings
Holy Spirit	The Spirit of God–in Hebrew *Ruach Hakodesh*
Trinity	God
Pentateuch	*Torah*
Friday evening prayer	*Kabbalat Shabbat*
Saturday evening prayer	*Havdalah*
Disciples	***Talmidim***

In a Jewish ministry, contextualization is not so difficult because the people of Israel are the people of the Hebrew Scriptures, the first part of the Bible. The worldview of the Jewish people is biblical, their stories are the stories of the Bible, their songs are composed of Psalms, their music and even dances are in harmony with the biblical principle of modesty, their rituals (*talith, tephilin,* prayers, immersion, etc.) are from the Bible.

Jewish ministry means to use an appropriate language, meaning there are some words to avoid, some others to replace by friendly Jewish words. Table 1 gives some examples of this vocabulary.

Summary

This chapter outlines the practical purpose of this dissertation, which is divided between a theoretical overview of the contextualized mission to the Jews, a historical overview of the anti-Semitism to which Jews have been subjected by Christian churches and the obstacles that this history has erected in preaching Yeshua.

I have made some suggestions in this chapter related to the church and theology. Some of these very specific suggestions should be seen in the context of my change plan in the previous chapter. I will work with my coalition group to grapple with these questions and seek answer to the problem of changing peoples' perspectives about the Jews and their relationship to Christianity.

In the next (and last) chapter I will present a general conclusion that contains recommendations for tactical shifts in mission work and a strategy for organizing a more efficient Gospel message in the Jewish community

CHAPTER 8

GENERAL CONCLUSIONS AND RECOMMENDATIONS

In this general conclusion I would like to give some recommendations for leading the Christian mission community towards a context-sensitive theology and ministry, which I call a friendly theology. This does away with Christianity's historic anti-Jewish tendencies that have unconsciously infected the image of Yeshua and the Church. This theology calls for respect for the Jewish people, her covenant, and the irrevocable gift and calling of the Lord towards the people of God of the Hebrew Scriptures. A friendly theology is a theology that recognizes the plan of God for the Jewish people, which is to bring them to the "new" covenant and to help them to recognize Yeshua as the Messiah of Israel, rather than trying to "dissolve" the Jewish identity. This "new" covenant should be understood in the context of Jeremiah 31: 31-34, which is a continuation and transformation of the covenant described in the Hebrew Scriptures. Yeshua is the divine mediator in a spiritual lineage going back to Aaron and his descendants, promising an interior transformation to believers, according to the verse: "The Kingdom of Heaven is within you" (Luke 17:21). From this perspective, the Jewish Yeshua is the very crown of Jewish history.

Friendly theology entails friendly and loving behavior towards Jews, in which Yeshua is at the center of a faith that gives comfort and reconciliation to the Jews. If we are to preach the Gospel to the Jews, we must preach a Biblically founded, contextualized Gospel. This contextualization will not only be About the message, but also about how to practice Christianity by accepting Jewish rituals and practices in the synagogues as long as they are in harmony with the Apostolic writings and do not deny Yeshua and his ministry of salvation for Israel and for the world.

Recommendations for an Effective Jewish Ministry

There are several ways to be effective in our ministry to Jews, and this practical dimension is one to which I turn in this last part of the dissertation, outlining some very important recommendations.

Jews Do not Lose Their Jewishness

My research confirmed a universally agreed upon point in the literature: Jews are proud of their Jewishness, and do not want to lose their identity. Why should they? A mission of contextualization sends the message that Jews who come to Yeshua are coming to a Jewish Messiah who will strengthen their Jewishness, and whose teaching is fully conformable to the Torah and Hebrew Scriptures. Yeshua is Israel's Messiah, the great hope announced by the prophets.

Jews Complete Their Destiny in Jesus

It is essential to share these Gospel stories for one's own Christian context as well. The story of Yeshua and his disciples is foundational and paradigmatic. As Bosch says, "It nourishes and challenges us in the present. Faith, is realized in *contemporaneity*, which means that there is, in the final analysis, no absolute discontinuity between the history of Jesus and the life of the church" (Elofer 2009, 145, 146). This continuity, not supersessionism, should be the overwhelming message of the Mission to the Jewish community. That Mission works best when the continuity between Judaism and Messianic Judaism (not a rupture) is made the basis of theory and practice. This requires a humble and contrite spirit, admitting the deviation of supersessionism and its departure from the message of the Gospels. The model of Paul and the other first disciples should be the model of the contemporary apostles to the Jews.

They Should Be Allowed to Practice the *Mitsvot*

It is more and more common to find Jews who believe in Yeshua and who claim to be Jewish-Christian or Messianic. These Jews, who see themselves in communion with their Jewish brothers and sisters, are faithful to their culture and to the Hebrew Bible. This means that they are faithful to the teaching of the Torah, to the mitzvoth, and other Jewish/biblical traditions.

A messianic body organized a conference called "the Helsinki Consultation" they met on June 29-July 2, 2012 in Berlin, Germany. The theme was "Jewish Believers in Yeshua and the Torah." These Messianic scholars affirmed the following statement[1]:

> We as Jewish believers in Yeshua acknowledge the special bond that unites us with Israel's Torah. This bond with Israel's Torah witnesses in the Church to the irrevocability of God's gifts and call to Israel (Rom 11:29). For Yeshua said, "Think not that I have come to destroy the Torah, or the prophets: I have not come to destroy, but to fulfill" (Mt 5:17). We believe in the continuing validity of the Torah even as it is fulfilled in Christ. Moreover, we see Christ as the incarnate Torah, the eternal wisdom of the Father in human flesh. He alone lived out the Torah in perfect form, and he calls his disciples to walk in his ways (Bosch 1984, 20)

It has only been in the last sixty years that there has emerged, in Judaism, a form of belief that accepts Yeshua in radically Jewish terms. These terms involve keeping the Torah while affirming Yeshua as the Messiah. Perhaps one of the factors in this movement was the miraculous emergence of the State of Israel. For example, Pinchas Lapide saw this connection:

---

[1] http://www.helsinkiconsultation2012.org/index.php/en/ (accessed September 10, 2012).

For Lapide, however, the most significant historical circumstance that has influenced the present course of Jewish attitudes toward Jesus and historical Jesus research is the founding of the modern state of Israel. In Lapide's view, the climate of Jewish independence and safety cultivated by the founding of the state of Israel—one in which Jews need neither tolerate nor fear Christian pressure—has led an unprecedented number of Jewish scholars to begin to look at Jesus anew and in a much more positive light. And though it is unique to Israel, Lapide contends that this free mental climate has also impacted Jewish scholars living outside of the physical boundaries of the relatively young country, positively influencing them toward similar endeavors (2010-2012).

It is not incompatible to accept Yeshua as the Messiah and to practice some Jewish *mitsvot* that are from the Bible.

Worshipping in Their Own Context

The above outlines the historical conditions that have led up to the critical contextualization of Jewish Messianism. The old anti-Judaic Christian bias sought to erase the converts ties to Judaism. However, since 1945, churches are increasingly accepting the fact that there is no valid biblical reason to strip Jews of their culture in order for them to recognize Yeshua as savior. More and more Messianic Jews are leaving traditional denominational fellowships in order to form specifically Messianic congregations. Some are organized as synagogues, and some go in other directions. The *Messianic Times* lists in their website[2] about 222 Messianic congregations in the world. The Messianic Israel Alliance[3] lists about 130 congregations affiliated with their alliance. The Word Jewish Adventist Friendship Center lists about fifty Jewish Adventist congregations in the world.[4] In fact, just in the United States there are about sixteen world Messianic organizations (see appendix E). Thousands of Messianic congregations are in existence all over the world today. This phenomenon is irreversible and will only

---

[2] http://www.messianictimes.com (accessed January 17, 2013)

[3] http://www.messianicisrael.com (accessed January 17, 2013)

[4] www.jewishadventist.org (accessed January 17, 2013)

grow in the coming years. For the sake of the mission, traditional denominations must learn to accommodate this phenomenon with contrite hearts, instead of opposing to it with old biases.

Jewish Practices Are not Syncretism

The fact that the rituals and practices of the Jewish people are biblical is a great difference with the other non-Christian world religions.

The *Talith* or shawl of prayer fulfills the commandment given in the Torah, "Speak to the Israelites and say to them: 'throughout the generations to come you are to make tassels on the corners of your garments, with a blue cord on each tassel. You will have these tassels to look at and so you will remember all the commands of the LORD" (Num 15:38–39). Jews are not to have these tassels on their clothes, but it is important for them to have this shawl of prayer with the tassels on the four corners.

The *Mezuzah* or *Mezuzoth* (plural) are ritual objects that fulfill a commandment. The Mezuzah is a small box containing some biblical texts, which is nailed to the doorframes of each entrance (house and rooms) in a Jewish home in order to fulfill another text of the Torah. "Write them on the doorframes of your houses and on your gates" (Deut 6:9). Thus, those who enter a believer's house know at once that this home reveres the name of the Lord.

The *Tephilin* are small black cubes with straps, which contain a parchment with biblical texts written on them. These cubes are tied to the forehead and the left arm (heart side) in order to fulfill the command that says, "Tie them as symbols on your hands and bind them on your foreheads" (Deut 6:8).

The Shabbat is not only ordained in one of the Ten Commandments (Exod.20:8-11), but is also, for the Jewish people, the commemoration of creation (Gen 2:1-3)

Jewish feasts commemorate Jewish history, like the French who celebrate their revolution on July 14, or the American 4th of July. Jews celebrate *Pesach* (Passover) as the day they received their freedom from Egypt. *Shavuot* (Pentecost) is the celebration of the gift of the Torah in Sinai. *Succoth* (the Tabernacle Feast) is the commemoration of their stay in the desert and the fact they lived in "tabernacles" or "tents" for forty years. These feasts celebrate Jewish history and faithfulness to the Hebrew Scriptures, and were important parts of Yeshua's life as a Jew. The Messianic congregations and synagogues understand these facts and encourage Jews to be faithful to their Holy Scriptures and to the God of Israel. Traditional Christian denominations should not look askance at this phenomenon.

Summary

In conclusion I would say that contextualization is a matter not only of praying and worshipping in the Jewish or synagogue style, but also of presenting the message of the gospel as good news for the Jewish people. The Mission to the Jewish community must be also about presenting Yeshua as a Jew to the Jews.

www.ingramcontent.com/pod-product-compliance
Lightning Source LLC
Chambersburg PA
CBHW051435290426
44109CB00016B/1571